MEN-AT-ARMS SERIES

EDITOR: MARTIN WINDROW

Wellington's Infantry (1)

Text and colour plates by

BRYAN FOSTEN

OSPREY PUBLISHING LONDON

Published in 1981 by
Osprey Publishing Ltd
Member company of the George Philip Group
12−14 Long Acre, London WC2E 9LP
© Copyright 1981 Osprey Publishing Ltd
Reprinted 1982, 1984, 1985 (twice), 1986, 1987,
1988

ISBN 0 85045 395 X

Filmset in Great Britain
Printed in Hong Kong

Author's Note:
**This book is the first of two volumes: the
second is planned for publication in November
1981. In this book the colour plates are devoted
to Foot Guards and 'English' Line Infantry
uniforms. The text describes the
establishments, composition, organization,
daily life, drill, and weapons and equipment of
the British infantry of the Napoleonic Wars. In
the second volume the colour plates will be
devoted to Rifles, Light Infantry and Highland
uniforms; and the text will describe and
illustrate in fuller detail the different items of
dress worn by the infantry as a whole.**

Composition of the Infantry

In 1763 the infantry comprised three regiments of Foot Guards, 124 'marching regiments of Foot', and a few Fencible regiments—in all, some 150 battalions.[1] In addition there were overseas a number of Provincial and similar units raised before or during the Seven Years' War. The return of peace brought inevitable disbandments, and the only permanent additions to the subsequent new establishment were the 50th to 70th Regiments of Foot.

The outbreak of the War of American Independence saw a further expansion of the infantry to 105 regiments, the last being the so-called 'Volunteers of Ireland' raised in North America but subsequently taken into the Line in 1782. Several regiments received second battalions; and in addition the war produced more than 90 Provincial (American loyalist) corps, ranging in importance from one unit with only 40 members, to the very strong Queen's Rangers, taken into the Line in 1782 with 1,000 officers and men, and De Lancey's Brigade, with a strength of 1,750.

The end of this war saw the infantry again reduced, this time to 75 regiments by 1785. When Britain went to war with Revolutionary France in 1792 the arm was expanded to 135 regiments plus many more second battalions. For example, in 1793 the following battalions were raised: 1 and 2/78th; 79th to 88th inclusive; 91st, 93rd, 94th, 95th; and 102nd. In 1794 they were augmented by the 2/81st, 2/82nd, 1 and 2/90th, 2/91st, 92nd, 2/94th, 97th, 99th, 100th and 101st; and by single-battalion regiments numbered 103rd to 130th and 132nd to 134th inclusive. The following year the 2/7th, 2/83rd, 5/60th, 131st and 135th were commissioned, and in 1800 the 95th (Rifles) (Coote-Manningham's).

In addition, many French émigré and other foreign regiments were raised for service, together with a German Legion largely based upon exiled Hanoverian troops. There was a corresponding expansion of the Militia and Volunteer establishments. The Regular Militia was a conscripted force of infantry, levied by ballot, supplementary to the Regular Establishment for which it was intended to provide reinforcements. Each county was responsible for raising its own force out of funds provided by the local rates. Command of the

Infantry shako of the type worn between *c.*1800 and 1806—the first, heavy leather pattern of this cap. The back 'fall', extended here, was normally folded up and hooked in place. (National Army Museum—as are all other illustrations not specifically credited to other sources)

---

[1] Fencible units were regular battalions, but raised for home service only, and solely for the duration of the conflict in question.

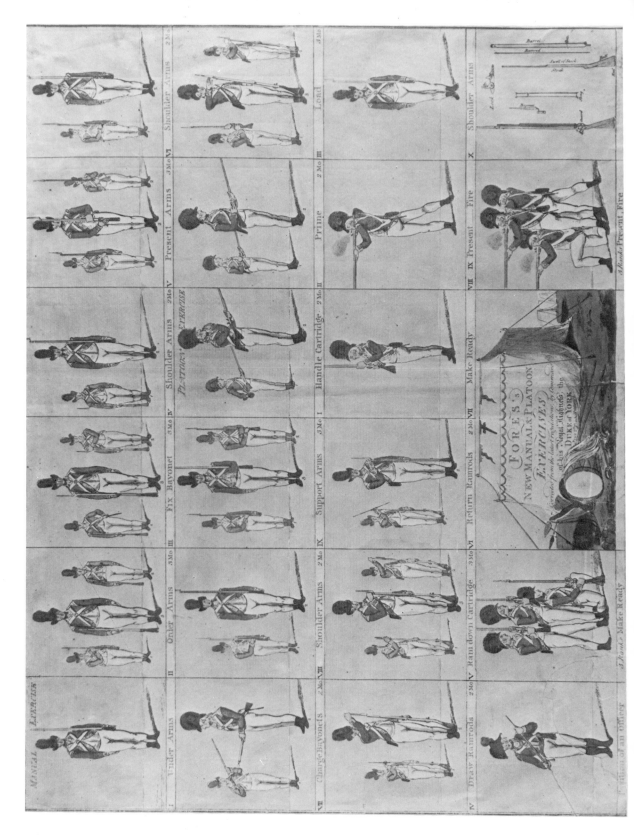

Fores's *New Manual Exercises* of 1798. The figures are light infantry company soldiers wearing the 'round' hat with a fur roach or crest. The jacket is the double-breasted type with exposed lapels of facing colour, cut away over the stomach. Note the dark (green?) feather in the cocked hat of the officer, bottom left; he too wears a short-tailed jacket.

4

county forces was vested in the Lord-Lieutenant. In 1815 Hamilton Smith produced charts identifying 71 units in Great Britain and 38 in Ireland; there were also three regiments on Guernsey and two companies on Sark. The Militia became 'embodied' when it was called out for permanent duties and organized into bodies capable of taking the field; and in the 1790s this was done. Special Acts were passed enabling militiamen to be 'pressed' into the regular Line regiments and to serve overseas; one of 1798 also promised a large bounty to recruits, but failed to achieve worthwhile results.

The Local Militia was the reserve force of the Militia proper, comprising small rural companies, and sometimes larger units, of rank and file with a few NCOs and one or two officers, usually local gentry. They were also raised by ballot, for periods of four years; unlike Regular Militia, they were not allowed to escape service by means of providing substitutes, and had to serve personally.

The Volunteers were privately raised units of patriotic citizens subsidised by local magnates and associations. In 1806 the force had 328,956 officers and men in units which bore the name of their neighbourhoods followed by 'Infantry' or 'Volunteers'—e.g. Clapham Volunteers. With few exceptions the Volunteer units were disbanded in 1813.

Under subsequent Acts second battalions were raised for many existing regiments: e.g., in 1802 for the 3rd, 18th, 26th, 30th, 39th, 42nd, 44th, 47th, 53rd, 57th, 58th, 61st, 66th, 67th, and 92nd. A similar Act of 1803 gave second battalions to the 5th to 10th inclusive, 14th, 15th, 21st, 23rd, 24th, 25th, 27th, 31st, 32nd, 36th, 38th, 40th, 43rd, 45th, 50th, 52nd, 56th, 59th, 62nd, 63rd, 71st, 72nd, 83rd, 87th, 88th, 89th, and 96th. The 1st Foot (Royal Scots) were granted an additional—third—battalion, and added a fourth later; while the 4th and 27th each received third battalions.

In 1797 six regiments—the 9th, 16th, 22nd, 34th, 55th and 65th—were given leave to recruit boys under 18½ years of age, offering a special bounty. Many of these recruits were barely in their teens, and consequently these units became known as the 'Boy Regiments'.

The effective infantry strength rose by a factor of three between 1793 and 1801, and the three

Infantry shako of the type worn between c.1806 and 1812. This is the lighter pattern made of felt, but in this case it has been laquered for protection; note the area exposed at top left, and the layered peak construction. The plate is of the universal pattern, though regimental differences of detail are recorded. Regimental numbers were sometimes stamped into the spaces at the 'shoulders' of the plate.

regiments of Foot Guards were similarly strengthened. Oman gives the infantry a rise from 31,379 to 117,953 men, and the Foot Guards from 2,885 to 8,725. The overall strength of the infantry in 1803 was 126,677 (privates and corporals—add approximately one-eighth for senior NCOs and officers).

From 1792 county titles were officially bestowed on the numbered infantry regiments not already in possession of particular designations. However, they also continued to be referred to officially by their colonels' names, especially in Parliamentary sources, until at least 1803. Colonels were given special injunctions to create positive links with the counties associated with their regiments.

Most major Army reforms between 1795 and 1803 were the direct result of the work of Prime Minister William Pitt and of Frederick, Duke of York, the Commander-in-Chief, following the disastrous campaigns in Holland; Sir John Fortescue gives his opinion that these changes were the most significant in the history of the Army up to that time.

Commanders and Staff

When war broke out with the French Republicans there was no true commander-in-chief of the Army. Lord Amherst had been the so-called 'General-on-the-Staff' between 1778 and 1782, and held the same appointment between 1793 and 1795 but, in most respects, it was Pitt who formally created the triumvirate of Secretary of War, Under-Secretary of State for War, and Commander-in-Chief. From about 1798 the Secretary of War became responsible for the Colonies; and in April 1798 the Duke of York was appointed Commander-in-Chief.

The Duke of York's Reforms

HRH Frederick Augustus, Duke of York and Albany, KG, the second son of King George III, had been a Field-Marshal for three years; in 1798

Infantry shako of 1812 pattern worn by an officer of the light infantry company of the 33rd Foot, later the Duke of Wellington's Regiment, at Waterloo in 1815; note the shot holes. It retains on the front a bugle horn badge above the cut-out numbers '33'; the edge of the former can just be seen.

he was 35 years of age. At 16 he had been sent by his father to Berlin to study the art of war under Frederick the Great. He proved a good student, and returned home with many sound, practical ideas. He was given command of the British contingent in the campaigns in the Low Countries in 1793 and 1794 and, probably unjustly, received much of the blame for its poor showing. The famous nursery rhyme became popular at that time as a cynical broadsheet commentary on his leadership.

Although the Duke became the scapegoat for many of the Army's shortcomings, they were actually of long standing. He was not the best of field commanders, and there seems little doubt that his talents lay in the field of administration and reform. His most important achievement was the restoration of discipline and morale in the officer corps.

The British force in Holland received scathing criticism from foreign military observers and Allied commanders. There were damning comments on the appalling behaviour of officers, their lack of care for their men and their generally drunken demeanour. The Army as a whole showed up badly in the field. The drill manuals were out of date, the battalions were of poor quality, there was little or no effective commissary or medical support, and uniform clothing was old-fashioned and of disgraceful quality. The men were prone to ill-discipline, mainly because of their conditions, and the fact that the time they had to serve overseas was far too long—ten years abroad for every five served at home. Some units had been abroad in foreign stations for more than 20 years.

The Duke set himself the daunting task of curing these problems as quickly as possible, and there is little doubt that during his term of office much was achieved—by the standards of that time. Field and manual exercises were revised; strict codes of behaviour for officers and senior NCOs were introduced; medical services were improved; and the Treasury was coerced into giving the Com-

Pyne's Camp Scenes, 1803. Top left, a woman wearing a uniform jacket is dressing her man's queued hair. Centre right, the men clean and press their jackets; bottom right, they are being shaved. There are several examples here of a crescent-shaped fatigue cap, apparently worn 'fore and aft' and pulled down square on the head.

Drawn & Etch'd by WH Pyne

London Published May 1 1803 by Pyne & Nattes

Infantry shako of 1812–16 pattern, worn by an officer at Waterloo. The cord or 'garland' of gold and crimson is unhooked here—the ring at the end was sewn to the left side matching that on the right, and the cockade and feather tuft were fixed above it. Note the laquered rear 'fall' neatly folded and hooked in place.

Besides being Commander-in-Chief, the Duke was created Captain-General of the Armed Services in Great Britain and all forces of the Crown employed in Europe, although the Home Secretary retained control of the Militia, Volunteers and Yeomanry Cavalry.

The Duke reduced the number of infantry regiments to around 100, and made the battalions of uniform strength; formed depôt companies to facilitate training and recruiting; and transformed inefficient battalions into second battalions for stronger existing regiments. He also helped create a better General Staff structure linking his office at the Horse Guards, Whitehall, with generals commanding armies, districts, brigades and divisions. He helped raise the Royal Staff Corps with a strength of five companies. A superior technical Staff body, this served Abercromby in Egypt, and came into its own in the Peninsula where it blossomed into a highly efficient corps under the Duke of Wellington. In addition the Duke of York saw to the formation of the Royal Waggon Train from the cumbersome Corps of Waggoners and Drivers—also known as the 'Newgate Blues'—and generally considered to be a rascally crew of blackguards.

Under the Commander-in-Chief were two main military branches of the General Staff: the Departments of the Adjutant-General and the Quartermaster-General, each with an establishment of Deputies, Assistants and Deputy-Assistants. The C-in-C himself had a staff consisting of a military secretary, aides-de-camp and brigade majors, and commanders in the field had similar support.

The Adjutant-General was responsible for all matters relating to discipline, regulation arms and clothing; the QMG, for the provision of certain stores, quartering, marches, movements and intelligence. Financial matters came under the control of the Treasury, which also controlled the provision of food, forage and transport via the Commissariat. A subsidiary of the Treasury was the Paymaster-General's office, which dealt with pay; this was delivered, often tardily, to the battalions under the auspices of Agents who acted as regimental bankers. In addition a specially convened Board of General Officers was responsible for the inspection and selection of all

missariat a better formal structure than the old, out-moded Corps of Captain-Commissaries and Drivers. Additional measures were introduced to improve and standardise much of the uniform clothing.

uniforms and equipment which were approved under sealed pattern by the Sovereign.

There remained the Board of Ordnance, an ancient traditional body which was a law unto itself, controlling the design and manufacture of artillery and firearms of all kinds. The Duke considered it an inefficient body.

In the early 1790s there were few purpose-built barracks in England, although more existed in Ireland, and fortified farms and manor houses were used in Scotland. Large bodies of troops had to be quartered in alehouses, farms, and domestic dwellings provided by local watch committees. In 1792 the post of Barrackmaster-General was created, the first incumbent being a Deputy Adjutant-General, to launch a major programme for the construction of barrack blocks at selected points throughout the United Kingdom. One hundred such establishments, mostly of poor standard, were built within the first 25 years of the 19th century, enabling the Army to develop from a loosely-knit force depending entirely on an *ad hoc* civilian-based quartering system into an efficient and self-sufficient organization totally housed in specially provided cantonments.

In 1799 the Duke of York was further responsible for the formation of a school for aspiring young Staff officers at High Wycombe, and personally selected the first 30 pupils. This later became the Staff College. He is also said to have been mainly responsible, during much the same period, for the formation of a Royal Military School at Great Marlow.

In March 1809, due to indiscretions by his mistress who had been corruptly selling commissions, the Duke was forced to resign. His successor was Sir David Dundas, QMG between 1796 and 1803. Dundas was elderly and tentative and much less effective in office than the Duke; the Army heaved a collective sigh of relief when the Duke was re-instated in 1811, remaining in the post until 1827.

In 1806 William Pitt died, and in the ensuing political upheaval William Wyndham assumed responsibility for the War Department. In April of that year he determined that the compulsory aspects of recruitment, and drafts via the Militia as a result of the Additional Forces Acts, should cease; thereafter enlistment should be on a purely voluntary basis. To encourage recruiting it was decided to make the Army more attractive and additional measures were introduced. Henceforth each two years' service in the dreaded West Indies counted as three years of normal service; pensions were introduced; and men were per-

Shako of the 92nd Highlanders, of the 1806–12 pattern. This appears to be an officer's undress cap worn as an alternative to the Highland bonnet. The tuft and cockade are missing from the central top edge; the regimental sphinx badge is worn in place of the regulation infantry plate. Note leather peak, good-quality felt crown, and ribbed silk ribbons worn as chin tapes. The 28th Regiment retained this pattern of cap, complete with back and front plates, during the Waterloo campaign.

Burnished brass soldier's breastplate of the 58th Foot; officers wore a similar but gilded pattern between 1800 and 1816. Some regiments wore rectangular plates.

mitted to enlist for short periods rather than for life. There were three successive enlistment periods, each being of seven years in the infantry, and each re-enlistment attracted higher pay.

Apart from the influence of the Duke of York, several general officers in the field influenced the development of infantry and tactics during the period. The most important was Arthur Wellesley, Duke of Wellington; but Sir John Moore's important part in the development of Light Infantry and Rifle Corps, and the trust and affection which were given to Sir Ralph Abercromby by all the troops under his command, also materially affected the development of the British infantry.

Wellington

It is obviously impossible to give more than the briefest summary here of the man whose professional and personal dominance over the British Army in a critical period had such enormous results, for the Army, Britain, and Europe at large; excellent biographies are readily available. It

should perhaps be mentioned, however, that his predominance among British military figures of the Napoleonic era is so far beyond challenge that the form we have chosen for the title of this book and future companion volumes will, we feel sure, be accepted as entirely just and natural.

Arthur Wellesley, third surviving son of the second Lord Mornington, was probably born on 30 April or 1 May 1769—the exact day and place are slightly obscure. His family were minor and impoverished Anglo-Irish aristocrats; as a boy he was considered to be quite without promise. He went to Eton, and from there to the Military Academy at Angers, France, where he was instructed by strategists including Pignerol. (At the same period Napoleon Bonaparte, also born in 1769, was a student at the Academy at Brienne.) On 7 March 1787 Wellesley was gazetted an ensign in the 73rd Foot, and on 25 December the same year he was promoted to a lieutenancy in the 76th. Shortly afterwards he served for some time with the cavalry, in both the 12th and 18th Light Dragoons. In April 1793 he obtained his majority in the 33rd Foot, and in September the same year he became its lieutenant-colonel; this rapid progress from ensign to lieutenant-colonel was obtained by the usual purchase system of that period.

His active service began in May 1794 when he went to Flanders with the Duke of York, and he later commanded the rearguard during the retreat to the River Waal. On his return to England, deeply disturbed by the sights he had seen in Flanders, he worked hard to bring the 33rd up to a higher standard of efficiency, and to improve his own professional education. Posted to the West Indies in the spring of 1795, he was obliged to return when the fleet sustained storm damage. He was with his regiment at Poole until April 1796, when he was granted the colonelcy and the regiment was posted to the East Indies. In February 1797 the 33rd was on the Bengal establishment.

Wellesley served with dedication and distinction in India until 1805. His elder brother's appointment as Governor-General of India in 1798 helped him to advantageous commands, but his success in them was due to his own growing professionalism. In 1799 he commanded a division in the campaign against Tipoo Sahib, Sultan of Mysore, and was made governor after the capture of the Sultan's capital, Seringapatam. Promoted major-general in May 1802 after further action against the Mahrattas, he achieved his first major victory in an independent command at Assaye in September 1803. With 1,800 British and 5,200 native troops and 22 guns, he defeated 40,000 Mahrattas with 100 guns. After another victory at Argaon he was knighted in 1804.

Although much fêted in India, at home he was just another 'sepoy general', and a very junior one. In late 1805 he commanded a brigade under Cathcart in the abortive expedition to Hanover; and next saw action at Copenhagen in August 1807, where his Reserve Brigade of excellent light troops captured Kjöge. In 1808 he was promoted lieutenant-general, and sailed for Portugal; there he was to lead some 17,500 men on a vaguely defined mission, undertaking operations against the French occupiers of the Iberian Peninsula. Between 1808 and 1814 (with one short absence) he led the Peninsular Field Army in a series of escalating victories, which made his name a household word, and raised the professional reputation of the British Army to a level unknown since Marlborough. Created Viscount Wellington of Talavera for his victory outside that town in 1809, he returned home in June 1814 to a hero's welcome.

After a year of diplomatic missions at the highest level he took command of the Anglo-Allied army in the Waterloo campaign of June 1815. Here he fought Napoleon in person for the first time; and here the lessons he had learned during the long Peninsular campaigns bore their final fruit. The British infantry fought in their usual exemplary style, and held the field until evening brought the Prussians, and the final rout of the French. It is alleged that as Napoleon left the field he turned to his aide, Gen. Comte de Flahaut, and exclaimed, 'It has always been the same, ever since Crécy!'

The infantry was Wellington's favoured tool, and he played a major rôle in raising its standards of excellence. He used it carefully, on ground which he selected to give it maximum advantage and protection; and he came to understand its capabilities and weaknesses exactly. A strict disciplinarian, he knew when to turn a blind eye. He asked a great deal from his men, but always tried to ensure that they had the equipment, the training and the officers they deserved. He introduced reforms which improved their career structure and their comfort and health alike. He never bullied them over pointless details, but insisted on the highest standards of professional behaviour in the field. He was nearly always outnumbered and far from reinforcements; it became his invariable habit to use his men's lives sparingly, and in return he gained their trust—though never the sentimental affection they had given Moore or Abercromby.

Establishment

In March 1806 the strength of the infantry was approximately 160,000 officers and men, including the large and prestigious King's German Legion. In 1807 the bounty for a militiaman transferring to the regular Line was £10, and an

Officer's sword belt breastplate of the 33rd Foot, of the pattern worn from 1800 to 1815; after that date the silver plate had the word WATERLOO **added beneath the Garter.**

Gorget, 1812—the insignia of an officer on duty. The universal pattern was gilded, and worn suspended on 'petersham' silk ribbons of the facing colour, which passed through the holes in the tips and ended in large rosettes.

ensigncy was given to any Militia officer who brought 40 volunteers with him.

1809 Establishment

In 1809 there were 25 1st Bns. and 42 2nd Bns. serving in the United Kingdom, together with three 3rd Bns.—although the 3/1st Foot had been at Walcheren and was with Moore at Corunna.

Eleven 1st Bns., 15 2nd Bns. and one 3rd Bn. served with the Peninsular Army; of these the 1/43rd, 1/52nd and 1/95th Rifles had been with Moore.

There were 10 1st Bns., three 2nd Bns. and one 3rd Bn. in Sicily with Sir Charles Stuart. Two 1st Bns. served at Gibraltar, and two 1st and two 2nd Bns. on Madeira.

Twenty-one 1st Bns. and two 2nd Bns. were in the East Indies; in the West Indies were 21 1st Bns., two 2nd Bns., and four 3rd Bns.; four 1st Bns. were at the Cape of Good Hope, and a further six 1st Bns. were in Canada and Nova Scotia. Two 1st Bns. served in New South Wales.

The deployment produced a total of 179 active battalions, which varied in strength from unit to unit and from time to time. Examples are the 1st

Foot, the Royal Scots, with four battalions totalling 4,926 all ranks; the 7th Fusiliers, with two battalions totalling 2,031; the 23rd Fusiliers, with two battalions and 2,079; the 32nd Foot, whose two battalions totalled 1,829; the 42nd Highlanders, with two battalions totalling 2,031; the seven battalions of the 60th Rifles, with 4,847; the 61st Foot, with two battalions and 1,820 men; the 88th Foot, with two battalions and 2,031; the 93rd Highlanders, whose two battalions totalled 1,820; the 101st Foot, with one battalion of 906; and the single-battalion 103rd Foot, with only 486 all ranks. This cross-section gives an average strength of 980 officers and men per battalion.

The three battalions of the 1st Foot Guards had 4,619 all ranks; the two battalions of the 2nd Foot Guards, 2,887; and the two battalions of the 3rd Foot Guards, 1,887. Both 1st and 2nd Foot Guards sent their flank companies to Walcheren, and detached companies of the 2/2nd and 2/3rd were sent to Cadiz in 1810.

In addition to the active regiments the establishment included Veteran and Garrison units; in 1809 there were 12 of the former and eight of the latter. Veteran Battalions varied in strength from 693 to 1,129 officers and men; the Garrison Regiments each had an establishment of 906. At one time there were as many as 16 Garrison and 13 Veteran units.

There were also several foreign corps in British service, including De Meuron's, De Natteville's, and De Roll's, besides several regiments named 'York' which seem to have had the character of penal units. Apart from these there were the French émigrés of the Chasseurs Britanniques; and Dutch, Italian, Corsican, Sicilian, Greek, Maltese and even Albanian corps. The excellent King's German Legion had ten infantry battalions, four of which—the 1st, 2nd, 5th and 7th—served in the Peninsula; the 3rd, 4th, 6th and 8th were in Sicily, and the 9th and 10th were stationed in the UK, although they served at Walcheren. Four of these battalions had strengths of 1,062 all ranks in 1809; the others had establishments of 962.

Horse Guards occasionally allowed active regiments of Foot to recruit foreigners; these were mostly Germans, or other Europeans who had been occupied by, or prisoners of, the French.

Recruitment of Frenchmen from the prison hulks was not encouraged. The foreigners serving King George included Poles, Dutch, Italians, Hungarians, Swedes, Danes, Russians, and even negroes, although the latter were normally seen in Bands of Music as 'Janissary Percussion' players.

British Infantry in the Peninsula: Effective Strength, January 1814 (unit strength in brackets):

1st Division (Lt.Gen. Sir John Hope) ... (8,230)
Maitland's Brigade: 1/1st Foot Guards (785); 3/3rd Foot Guards (776)
Stopford's Bde: 1/2nd FG (767); 1/3rd FG (864)
Hinuber's Bde: 1st Line Bn. KGL (574); 2nd Line Bn. KGL (532); 5th Line Bn. KGL (482); 1st Lt. Bn. KGL (568); 2nd Lt. Bn. KGL (585)
Aylmer's Bde: 1/62nd Foot (427); 76th (546); 77th (170); 85th (430); and from March 1814, 1/37th (strength not included).

2nd Division (Lt.Gen. Sir Rowland Hill) (6,270)
Barnes Bde: 1/50th (345); 1/71st (498); 1/92nd (391); 1 company 5/60th (49).
Byng's Bde: 2/31st Foot (271) and 1/66th (178) combined as 1st Provisional Bn.; 1 coy. 5/60th Rifles (45)
Pringle's Bde: 1/28th (485); 1/34th (410); 1/39th (565); 1 coy. 5/60th (47)
Harding's Bde: 6th and 8th Portuguese Line; 6th Portuguese Caçadores (total 1,918)

Unattached Portuguese Division
(Maj.Gen. Le Cor) ...   . (3,771)

Da Costa's Bde: 2nd and 14th Portuguese Line (total 1,802)
Buchan's Bde: 4th and 10th Portuguese Line; 10th Caçadores (total 1,969)

3rd Division
(Lt.Gen. Sir Thomas Picton)   ... (5,317)
Brisbane's Bde: 1/45th Foot (496); 1/74th (438); 1/88th (738); 4 coys. 5/60th Rifles (197)
Keane's Bde: 1/5th (640); 2/83rd (371); 2/87th (305); 1/94th (350)
Power's Bde: 9th and 12th Portuguese Line; 11th Caçadores (total 1,782)

4th Division
(Lt.Gen. Hon. Sir G. Lowry Cole) ... (5,389)
Anson's Bde: 3/27th Foot (564); 1/40th (468); 1/48th (413); 2nd Provisional Bn., partly 2/53rd (total 480); 1 coy. 5/60th Rifles (45)
Ross's Bde: 1/7th (604); 70th (395); 1/23rd (420); 1 coy. Brunswick-Oels (42)
Vanconcelle's Bde: 11th and 23rd Portuguese Line; 7th Caçadores (total 1,958)

5th Division
(Maj.Gen. Hon. C. Colville)   ... (3,597)

Hay's Bde: 3/1st Foot (320); 1/9th (482); 1/38th (364); 2/47th (256); 1 coy. Brunswick-Oels (25)
Robinson's Bde: 1/4th (344); 2/59th (268); 2/84th (294); 1 coy. Brunswick-Oels (20)
De Regoa's Bde: 2nd and 15th Portuguese Line; 8th Caçadores (total 1,224)

6th Division (Lt.Gen. Sir H. Clinton) ... (5,243)
Pack's Bde: 1/42nd Foot (669); 1/79th (594); 1/91st (458); 1 coy. 5/60th Rifles (37)

Officer's jacket of the 1st Bn., 60th (Royal American) Regiment. The 5th and 6th Bns. and the light infantry companies of the 1st–4th Bns. were dressed as Rifle corps in green, but this scarlet jacket with blue facings was the uniform of the senior battalions. The 60th were a 'non-laced' regiment. The silver buttons, set in pairs, bear '60' in a Garter with an inset Crown.

(Top) New Land Pattern musket, *c.*1805. See details in body of text. During the Peninsula campaigns light infantry browned the barrels of their muskets to kill the reflection—in bright sunlight the flash of bright barrels could quickly disclose the location of infantry to enemy scouts. The custom was copied by most infantry formations. (Bottom) India Pattern musket, *c.*1790. When stocks of muskets were reduced by excessive demand, orders for the 'East Indian' pattern were increased. Battalions shipping overseas were equipped either with the old 'Long' pattern or with the modified India type; most Militia units were equipped with the latter.

Lambert's Bde: 1/11th (477); 1/32nd (464); 1/36th (365); 1/61st (438)
Douglas's Bde: 8th and 12th Portuguese Line; 9th Caçadores (total 1,775)

Light Division (Maj.Gen. C. Alten) ... (3,925)

Kempt's Bde: 1/43rd Foot (724); 1/95th Rifles (422); 3/95th Rifles (365)
Colborne's Bde: 1/52nd (714); 2/95th Rifles (350)
plus 17th Portuguese Line; 1st and 3rd Caçadores (total 1,350)

Unattached:

Maj.Gen. Bradford's Bde: 13th and 24th Portuguese Line; 5th Caçadores (total 1,449)
Brig.Gen. Campbell's Bde: 1st and 6th Portuguese Line; 4th Caçadores (total 1,561)
Capt. Gibson: 13th Royal Veteran Bn. (871)

Army Life

Recruiting

A 'beating order' was obtained from the commanding officer of the battalion, and the sergeant-major was usually entrusted with the task of selecting men for the detail. The recruiting party consisted of an officer, two sergeants, a drummer, and from two to five men. Their orders were to 'beat up' an area. Members of the party were supposed to be picked for their smart appearance, to be 'chosen men' permitted to improve their uniforms by the addition of bunches of national-coloured ribbons, or favours, pinned to their caps. In reality many appear to have been elderly NCOs who could easily be spared, along with sub-standard privates. Experienced officers of avuncular manner were naturally chosen rather than hard-nosed, foppish subalterns. In such areas as Chatham, Portsmouth, Falmouth and Dover the recruiters steered well clear of the waterfront where the voracious naval press-gangs roved.

In 1808 there were 26 District Surgeons ready to check recruits; and during the whole period of the Napoleonic Wars doctors' 'surgeries' and martial recruiting parties were prominent features of life in cities, towns and villages: 'Drumming and fifing was heard in the streets from dawn until dusk . . .' The recruit saw the doctor after taking 'the King's shilling'. If he was passed fit—and most were—he received his bounty. This was usually about £2.12s.; it was increased in 1812, reduced in 1814, and increased again in 1815. From this sum he had to pay two guineas for his knapsack, leaving him only some 10s. from what had at first appeared a sizeable sum. Mustered under a sergeant, the party of recruits would then be marched off to the nearest depôt, where they were 'sized' and allocated to their companies.

They messed together, receiving two meals daily—breakfast and dinner. Drills began almost immediately, to the new standards laid down by the Duke of York. Mondays and Fridays were given over to Battalion Drill, Thursdays and Saturdays to Brigade Drill; Wednesdays were Field Days, and Thursday was the soldier's Day of Rest. They were drilled two or three times daily under the eye of tough NCOs; and this pattern lasted six or seven months. Once they had mastered the intricate drill movements they moved on to drilling with the musket, or 'firelock'.

Recruits were not allowed out of the depôt until after Tattoo, which was beaten at dusk. When their initial training was complete they were given the pay of a fully trained soldier, and their first regimental headdress. They were then considered fit for active service. However, training did not finish there; even after being posted to their permanent company 'home' they continued to receive regular drills wherever they were stationed, until they were finally posted overseas.

Clothing provided on enlistment varied, but in 1795 they were given linen trousers, waistcoats, and plain red 'slop' jackets in summer; in winter they were also given cotton drawers, and sleeved waistcoats of flannel. At a later date this 'slop' clothing was changed to 'a red jacket made to button all the way down, with a collar of the facings, and the button of the regiment, a short waistcoat lined with flannel, a pair of mixed-colour cloth trousers and a plain "round" hat and cockade' (WO/72/1795).

Age and Height

In 1793 Major Murdoch Maclean raised 100 men for the 98th Regiment. We are fortunate that he carefully recorded their ages and heights, giving us a neat break-down of what we may estimate are more or less typical percentages. The recruits ranged in age from 15 to 35 years. The highest percentage (33%) were between 30 and 35. There were 31% between 18 and 24; 19% between 25 and 29; and only 17% between 15 and 17.

Of the 100 men only three were 5ft. 10ins. or taller. Of the remainder, 23% were 5ft. 4ins., and 21% were below this height; 27% were 5ft. 6ins. to 5ft. 7ins. tall, and 16% 5ft. 7ins. to 5ft. 9ins.

A memorandum sent out by Horse Guards in 1809 concerning the standards of recruiting records that of 106 men on their list, eight were 5ft. tall; 15 were 5ft. 7ins.; 21 were 5ft. 4ins.; 28 were 5ft. 6ins.; 14 were 5ft. 10ins., and only one man was 6ft.—in other words, the majority were under 5ft. 6ins. tall.

The Foot Guards seem to have had the pick of the taller men. The average height of their grenadiers was 5ft. 11ins. in 1814. Battalion company men averaged 5ft. 7ins., and the Light

Officer's jacket of the 92nd Highlanders—a fine specimen of the service jacket of the Gordons. The buttons have '92' in a raised circle. The facings are yellow, and the lace has a black line in the silver, a regimental peculiarity. Note the tapered lengths and progressively slanted placing of the lace loops.

Rear of the Gordons officer's jacket. Note the thistle turnback ornaments, the small lace loops set on the false pocket flaps, and the triangle of lace at the waist.

Officer's jacket, 23rd (Royal Welch Fusileers) Regiment of foot, 1812; note elaborate gold edging and ornaments. Gold lace also lines the central vent and the pleats each side of it, though almost hidden inside the latter.

Infantry company, oddly enough, averaged 5ft. 8ins. tall.

Pay

The weekly pay of a 'private centinell' in 1797 was 7s. (seven shillings—35p. in modern currency, but this does not reflect its purchasing power, of course). Out of this he had to pay $1\frac{1}{2}$d. a day for his bread and meat. In all 4s. a week was taken for his messing, and another 1s.6d. was stopped for 'necessaries'. The remainder was paid to him, subject to his finding sufficient to pay for washing and cleaning his personal equipment. In camp and quarters he actually received about $5\frac{1}{4}$d. a week, which was the difference between the gross pay and the various stoppages. If the price of meat and bread exceeded 6d. a pound and $1\frac{1}{2}$d. a pound respectively the extra was paid by the authorities, up to a total of $\frac{3}{4}$lb. of meat and 1 lb. of bread daily.

Tables of Pay:

Rank	Foot Guards	Regiments of Foot
Colonel	£1.10s.6d.	£1.2s.6d.
Lt.Colonel	£1.1s.6d.	15s.11d.
Major	18s.6d.	14s.1d.
Captain	12s.6d.	9s.5d.
Lieutenant	6s.	5s.8d.
Ensign	4s.6d.	(2nd Lt.) 4s.8d.
Adjutant	10s.	8s.
Quartermaster	5s.3d.	5s.8d.
Surgeon	10s.	9s.5d.
Assistant Surgeon	7s.6d.	7s.6d.
Solicitor	3s.	?
Sergeant	1s.10$\frac{3}{4}$d.	1s.6$\frac{3}{4}$d.
Corporal	1s.4$\frac{3}{4}$d.	1s.2$\frac{1}{4}$d.
Private	1s.1d.	1s.
Drum Major	1s.10d.	?
Drummer	1s.2$\frac{1}{4}$d.	1s.1$\frac{3}{4}$d.
Musician	1s.6d.	?

The Paymaster received 2s.1$\frac{3}{4}$d. daily, a sergeant major 2s.0$\frac{3}{4}$d., a quartermaster sergeant 2s.0$\frac{3}{4}$d. and a paymaster sergeant 1s.6$\frac{3}{4}$d.

At the end of the 18th century a record was made of the items a soldier had to provide at his own expense: one pair of black cloth gaiters @ 4s.; one pair of breeches, besides those called 'ammunition breeches', @ 6s.6d.; one one-inch hair leather @ 2$\frac{1}{2}$d.; one worm, turnscrew, picker and brush for his musket every five years @ 1s.3d.; emery, brick dust and oil for keeping his metal bright @ 2s.6d. a year; and the cost of altering the watchcoats.

Barracks

The few early barracks had been virtually forts, situated mostly in Ireland and Scotland. Those constructed at the end of the 18th century were larger, but equally forbidding. Cheerless, prison-like buildings, they had no provision whatsoever for recreation, comprising little more than four walls containing sleeping quarters each providing soldiers with about 300 cubic feet of air per man. Twenty men were allocated a room seldom more than seven feet high, 30 to 32ft. long and 20ft. wide. Only about six inches separated the primitive 'cribs' from the central eating table.

In such rooms the soldiers ate, drunk and slept, four to a 'crib', sleeping on malodorous straw and covered by a few threadbare blankets. Their only light was from tallow dips, two to each room. In this atmosphere, foetid with stale sweat and pipe smoke, men might cluster round a literate comrade while he read from a book or broadsheet.

The only urinals were wooden buckets or tubs, of the kind also used for washing. Night soil was tipped into cesspits, around which the ground became poached and foul. Drinking water was meagrely provided from a single pump with a couple of buckets.

Sections of the barrack rooms were partitioned off by blankets slung on ropes to make 'married quarters', providing a minimal privacy for the men with wives. Here children were born, often with the father's comrades standing around watching and smoking clay pipes. Tuberculosis and rheumatism were rife.

With no recreation in the building the soldiers had no recourse but to visit alehouses and other dens in the town, where they got drunk on cheap gin—beer was comparatively expensive at that time. At a later date canteens were formed and sutlers were licensed; but many were rogues who sold bad liquor at high prices.

Food

The infantryman's diet was monotonous. The major basic commodity provided by the Commissariat was flour, made up by field bakeries into large loaves of coarse bread. This was supported, and often replaced in the field, by issues of thin, hard, round biscuits known as 'navy biscuits'—they were the same weevil-infested 'hardbakes' issued to sailors of the Fleet. The daily issue of 'ammunition bread' was about 1 or $1\frac{1}{2}$lb. per man. When neither bread nor biscuit were available they were often replaced by issues of rice, flour, or lentils. The bread ration was supplemented by $\frac{3}{4}$lb. of beef, when available. At intervals there were issues of peas, beans and local cheese.

Having bought his ration out of his subsistence it was usual for the soldier in the field to prepare it with a group of comrades, often accompanied by company women. The beef was sometimes boiled, sometimes simply broiled over a fire on a makeshift spit of twigs or ramrods. The biscuit was mostly crushed and dropped, along with stale bread, into water or the thin beef soup to make gruel. Peas, beans, lentils and rice were all added as available. When only the flour 'came up' it was rubbed with lard and formed into greasy dumplings which were also added to the pot. Soldiers

became expert at concocting more or less savoury messes from pounded biscuit and bread with added flavouring; this kind of improvised porridge was popularly known as 'stirabout'.

Poor as this food seems to us, it was better than that provided for the French soldier. Napoleon expected his men to live off the country by foraging, apart from a basic bread issue. Even this often depended on the army harvesting local crops. Although this gave the French greater manoeuvrability through a simplified logistic 'tail', it often proved disastrous. Licence to rob was all very well when advancing through a fat countryside in summertime, with poultry and pigs for the taking; on a hard winter retreat, or in a terrain deliberately stripped by the fleeing population, it could mean starvation. In contrast the British normally had something to eat, even if not very palatable or nourishing. There were, of course, exceptions at times of severe emergency, such as the retreat to Corunna.

Supplementary food and alcohol were available

Front view of the 23rd Foot officer's jacket opposite. This excellent example has a curious regimental cuff design. The fringed wings have bullion twist edging and 'darts' in curves across the shells. The convex gilded buttons bear the Prince of Wales's Plumes in a Garter with the regimental title below the Crown.

A canvas knapsack of *c.*1805, of the pattern carried until the introduction of the black box pattern designed by Trotter of Soho Square. It is coloured brown. Note the carefully painted and 'shadowed' patch bearing the title 'RBV'—presumably the initials of a Volunteer unit—above 'Gren.ʳ Comp.ʸ'. Line troops often had their regimental number painted on such a patch, apparently of facing colour.

from the sutlers. Each regiment had a 'grand sutler', a civilian contractor with a staff of assistants who sold extras at company level. Besides beer, wine or brandy they often contrived to provide vegetables, a necessary addition to the soldiers' diet if they were to avoid scurvy. Many prints of the period show sutlers' quarters in the background, usually open-fronted tents with a wagon tilt spread on poles to give overhead cover, and furnished with a few tables and benches. Soldiers are frequently depicted being served by women—whether members of the sutlers' teams or other camp followers it is difficult to say.

In the field there was certainly some issue of alcohol, though the details are rather obscure. The ration was supposed to be $\frac{1}{3}$ pint of rum or a pint of wine daily per man. Gin was often substituted; the famous memoirs of Sgt. Tom Morris describe his drawing dead men's gin rations on the field of Waterloo itself.

Bivouacs and Tents

Until the latter part of the Peninsular War there was no universal issue of tents to the Army. Consequently the troops became proficient at building temporary shelters from boughs, foliage, straw, and odd materials gathered at the nightly halts on the march. When they were halted at one place for some time these bivouacs became more sophisticated. Glieg records how he and his fellow officers adapted primitive peasant cottages by knocking holes through to temporary chimneys which they built against the outside walls. Officers usually monopolised available buildings when shelter was hard to find; but there is a record of the Duke of Wellington reacting furiously when he found that a group of them had put wounded men out into the night in order to take over their shelter. In occupied towns in the Peninsula soldiers and officers alike were billeted on local civilians.

Where no bivouac material was to be found the troops simply rolled up as best they could in their greatcoats and blankets, sometimes contriving crude but effective sleeping-bags. Many of Wellington's army spent the night before Waterloo lying in deep mud, or sitting on their knapsacks. In extreme conditions officers were no better off than their men, although some carried privately purchased tents around with them on campaign. There is one splendid memoir of an officer having his countryman soldier-servant 'thatch' him into a nest of bracken and weeds each night!

Drawings by St Clair and others give some indication of the variety of tents which became available after 1813. Some are simple bell tents designed to hold ten or a dozen men. These were issued on a company basis, as was a smaller tent with a horizontal ridge-pole which housed about five men. St Clair shows officers' tents to be more elaborate affairs, with flys and porches propped on poles.

Women and Marriage

Soldiers were discouraged from marrying, but many were already in that 'happy state' when they enlisted. Only five women per company could be taken on the ration strength and were allowed to accompany their husbands on overseas service. Selection was by ballot at the port of departure; and contemporary accounts give heart-rending descriptions of the distress of those unlucky in the draw. The unlucky ones were issued with a certificate from a Justice of the Peace in the area of embarkation to assist her and her family to return to her home town. The Overseer of the Poor of any place through which she travelled was directed to provide her with $1\frac{1}{2}$d. per mile for the number of miles to the next place, not exceeding 18 miles.

The wives who did manage to follow the battalions abroad did so through entire campaigns; they played an important part in camp life, washing, mending and cooking not only for their husbands but often for his comrades as well. By providing these small services for a handful of coppers many women who had no official status on the ration strength seem to have contrived to follow their sweethearts. Most seem to have been very loyal; there are records of them searching the battlefields for their men, and even carrying their wounded or exhausted menfolk on the march. When a husband was killed most seem to have been practical enough to marry another soldier in the company without delay, to protect their status, and there was seldom any shortage of applicants. The camp women came under military discipline, and any misbehaviour was ruthlessly punished by the Provost department.

Organization

The Battalion

At full strength this comprised a headquarters, eight battalion companies, and two flank companies—the grenadier or right flank, and light infantry or left flank companies.

The headquarters consisted of: one lieutenant-colonel; two majors (one called the Senior Major); one adjutant; one surgeon and two assistant surgeons; one quartermaster; one sergeant major; one staff sergeant paymaster; one sergeant armourer; one drum major; one corporal pioneer and ten pioneers.

Each company consisted of: one captain; two lieutenants or ensigns; two sergeants; three corporals; one drummer; in some battalions, one fifer; and 85 to 100 privates. (Foot Guards battalions had larger establishments.)

In practice these figures were seldom achieved. Examinations of the Orders of Battle for the Peninsular Army reveal that while the Foot Guards usually fielded around 1,000 men per battalion, the regiments of Foot varied from less than 500 to around 800.

The eight battalion companies were divided into four 'grand divisions' of two companies each; 16 'sub-divisions' or half-companies; or 32 sections. When the battalion was insufficiently strong it was split into 24 sections for the purposes of the march, rather than 32. The battalion could also be divided into two 'wings', the right and left.

The battalion (or 'centre') companies were numbered from right to left, 1 to 8, always identified by Arabic numerals. The sub-divisions were numbered e.g. '1/6th'—the first sub-division of the 6th Company. The files were also numbered e.g. '1, 2, 3', etc. The grenadier and Light companies were numbered separately but in the same fashion, with the addition of their title.

The Colours were usually placed between the 4th and 5th battalion companies in the front rank of the battalion line, each covered by an NCO (latterly, the 'colour sergeant') or by a steady man in the rear rank. There was another sergeant between the two Colours in the front rank, covered by a second in the rear rank and a third in the supernumerary rank. The sole function of these NCOs was to advance and direct the line of march when the battalion moved, and to protect the Colours with their pikes when the battalion was in action. In action several additional NCOs might

Tailor's drawing for an officer's jacket of the 1st Line Bn., King's German Legion. The cut is clearly shown. The jacket was to be of 'super fine scarlet cloth with darke blue lappels, cuffs and collar', 'white casimere skirt linings and turnbacks ditto', and 'white rattinett boddy lining'. Note triangle of lace at the waist, and turnback edging.

Officer's jacket of the 34th (Cumberland) Regiment of Foot, 1812; the hook-and-eye method of fastening the front when the lapels were turned back is clearly shown here, as are the thread twist buttonholes of a 'non-laced' regiment. The convex silver buttons have a simple incised '34'.

be detached from their companies to increase the Colour guard, or to replace casualties.

For details of the design of regimental Colours, see Men-at-Arms 78, *Flags of the Napoleonic Wars (2)*, by Terence Wise.

Weapons and Equipment

Muskets

Arms were provided by the Board of Ordnance from stocks held in the Tower and other armouries. 'Brown Bess' was the popular name given to the British infantry's most famous weapon. The name is first mentioned in early 18th century documents, but its origins are obscure. Some believe it derives from the German *buchse*, meaning rifle; others that it refers to the rich brown colour of the polished walnut stocks, or even to the browning of barrels at certain periods. There can be no doubt, however, on one score: that this flintlock musket, in various updated patterns and modified

guises, was the principal weapon of the British infantryman from 1730 to 1830, during the whole period when the redcoat won his world-wide reputation and laid the foundations of empire. In a form modified for percussion fire it was even used as late as the Crimean War.

The pattern which first figured in our period was the 'Long Land Pattern', with a 46in. barrel, a wooden ramrod held in place by three metal 'pipes', and a more elaborate 'tailpipe' where the ramrod slid into the stock. One sling swivel was fixed to the trigger guard, the second to the stock about midway between the two upper ramrod pipes. The weapon was furnished with a 17in. socket bayonet.

By about 1725 steel ramrods were being issued, and in about 1740 a 'Short Land Pattern' began to be issued. This was essentially unchanged apart from a 42in. barrel. Both 'Long' and 'Short' versions were soon in concurrent use, with either steel or wooden ramrods, the latter now with metal heads.

During the French-Indian Wars in America lighter and handier weapons were found to be necessary for forest fighting and irregular warfare. By 1765 the need for a shortened barrel was officially acknowledged and a warrant was issued specifying that in future all barrels were to be 42ins. long. The 'Short Land' thus became the standard infantry weapon until it was superseded in its turn by the 'New Land Pattern'—although, probably for economic reasons, much of the Army adopted the 'East Indian Land Pattern', with a 39in. barrel and plainer furniture, in the 1790s.

In 1802–03 the 'New Land Pattern' was formally introduced, although many of the 'East Indian' muskets continued to be used. The 'New Land' was an amalgam of the 'Short Land' and 'East Indian' patterns. It had a brass butt plate, a plain trigger guard, a steel ramrod, two ramrod pipes and an ornate tailpipe. The muzzle end of the stock had a metal cap. The barrel was 42ins. long and had a bayonet-locking stud at the muzzle, which doubled as a foresight. A later, improved version of the 'New Land' had a 39in. barrel, notched backsight, and a scroll or 'pistol grip' trigger guard; it was issued to some crack Light Infantry regiments, and is today sometimes referred to as the Light Infantry Musket; but in fact its issue seems generally to have been restricted to sergeants of Light Infantry regiments and of light companies within Line regiments.

In the field the British infantry enjoyed an advantage over their enemies in that they used a heavier ball. This had greater stopping power and caused more serious wounds, an advantage when fighting in line formation against troops advancing in column. The comparative shortness of the barrels of the later patterns made loading and firing easier and, according to Mercer, this was specially appreciated by shorter men. The use of the heavier ball had an additional advantage: the British could, at need, use captured French ammunition, but the French Charleville could not accept the British ball.

The infantry had learnt, as British soldiers always will, that there was a short cut to loading. The soldier could prime and close his pan, and then simply drop the powder, torn paper cartridge and ball into the barrel and jog them down into place by banging the butt on the ground, rather than ramming. This will seem strange to anyone with experience of firing muzzle-loading muskets today, given the relatively tight fit of a paper-wrapped ball in the bore; perhaps there is something we do not understand about the contemporary descriptions, for both Sergeant Lamb and Sergeant Cotton record that the method was prevalent. During the Peninsular War the French are described as having adopted this 'jogging' method on a wide scale. They also sometimes thrust their ramrods into the ground at their feet between loadings, to avoid repeatedly pulling them from the pipes and returning them; this was probably done by most soldiers of the day.

It is well known that the first volley, from muskets loaded without haste and in the officially prescribed manner, was the most destructive. The subsequent volleys were invariably less effective. Loading was hasty, fire discipline became ragged, and mishaps were common. Excited soldiers would often forget to remove their ramrods from the barrel and would fire them away; others might load several charges one on top of the other without firing, with fatal results when they did pull the trigger.

British infantry of the period were described as cool and well-disciplined in action. Oman reports:

'They loaded their pieces, ramming charge and bullet well home, and there was no loss of windage.' There are several contemporary accounts from French eye-witnesses and veterans of French columns moving forward to the sound of massed drums playing the *Pas de Charge*, with officers exhorting them onward with waving swords and hats on high, confronted by a wall of silent redcoats. When the range was right the order was given, the muskets came up as one, and the resulting volley would tear away the front of the French column, causing panic in the rear. The French infantry invariably knew what would happen, and there was seldom any marked enthusiasm to occupy the front of the column.

The British invariably fought in two ranks, the French in three. A British battalion of 600 men occupied a front of some 200 yards, but a French battalion in line would only cover about 135 yards: they were thus overlapped at each end, and

Field officer's epaulette of the 31st (Huntingdonshire) Regiment of Foot, *c*.1810. Silver lace and embroidery and bullion twist fringe, with gold crown. The order of February 1810 identified this as the badge of a lieutenant-colonel. In regiments of Foot all field officers, including those of Brevet rank, wore two epaulettes. Details of pattern and proportions varied slightly from example to example.

A long-skirted coatee worn by an officer of the 27th (Enniskillen) Regiment of Foot, 1810. The back is quilted across the shoulders. Again, this is a 'non-laced' regiment, with buttons set singly. They are gold, almost flat, with the 'castle' badge below ENNISKILLEN in an arc, and above '27'.

5ins. Length incl. bayonet: 6ft. 8ins. Weight: 10lb. 12oz. (with bayonet: 11lb. 13oz.)
Short Land Pattern Barrel: 3ft. 6ins. Bayonet: 1ft. 5ins. Length incl. bayonet: 6ft. 4ins. Weight: 10lb. 8oz. (with bayonet: 11lb. 9oz.)
East Indian Land Pattern Barrel: 3ft. 3ins. Bayonet: 1ft. 5ins. Length incl. bayonet: 6ft. 4ins. Weight: 9lb. 11oz. (with bayonet: 10lb. 11oz.)
New Land Pattern Barrel: 3ft. 6ins. Bayonet: 1ft. 5ins. Length incl. bayonet: 6ft. 4ins. Weight: 10lb. 6oz. (with bayonet: 11lb. 6oz.)
'Light Infantry' Pattern Barrel: 3ft. 3ins. Bayonet: 1ft. 5ins. Length incl. bayonet: 6ft. 1in. Weight: 10lb. 1oz. (with bayonet: 11lb. 1oz.)

Pikes

In February 1792 the cumbersome sergeants' halberds were abolished. Henceforth, until 1830, battalion company, grenadier company and fusilier sergeants carried pikes. The new weapon had a 9ft. ash staff with a spearhead which screwed into a steel socket, and a crosspiece made separately, like a German boarspear. The crossbar was intended to prevent the point penetrating too deeply. The blade was $12\frac{3}{4}$ins. long, the crossbar $5\frac{1}{2}$ins. wide, and the socket, with two ornamental ring-pieces, $4\frac{1}{2}$ins. deep from the crossbar to the point where two 9in. flanges projected down the sides of the staff for strength. The foot of the staff was shod with iron $2\frac{1}{4}$ins. deep, with similar flanges $2\frac{1}{2}$ins. long extending up the sides of the staff.

Swords

An order issued in May 1796 ordered infantry officers to carry uniform swords: a necessary order, since many regiments had procured swords of different—and sometimes indifferent!—patterns, as inspection reports make clear. (Even so, not all units observed the order: e.g. the 1st Foot, who continued throughout the Peninsular War to carry swords with blades resembling those of Scots broadswords.)

The 1796 pattern infantry sword had a brass knuckle-bow guard, a ball pommel and side shells, all gilded. The grip was covered with silver twisted wire; the blade was straight, blued, and made to cut and thrust. It was an inch broad at the shoulder and 32ins. long. Its leather scabbard, heelballed black, had a thin wooden lining, a

every British musket could be brought into action, giving greater immediate firepower. This had an even more devastating effect when British line faced French column; British muskets could be brought to bear on the face and both flanks of the head of the column, and the effect of 600 muskets firing into such a closely packed formation can hardly be imagined. The two-rank formation also tended to minimise casualties from artillery roundshot, of course; a cannon ball might take three to six men out of a three-rank line, but only two to four from a British line.

The basic characteristics of the different musket patterns were as follows; note that weights and dimensions of individual weapons varied somewhat:
Long Land Pattern Barrel: 3ft. 10ins. Bayonet: 1ft.

brass mouth fitting with a stud to engage a frog, and a brass chape.

In 1803 a new sword was prescribed. This had a lion's-head pommel, and a knuckle-bow guard incorporating the Royal Cypher. The blued blade was sharply curved; the gilded brass scabbard fittings included two suspension rings, as the sword was carried on slings rather than a frog. It seems that it was never carried by the majority of battalion company officers, but became popular with flank companies, especially light infantry, as well as with field officers and generals. Foppish officers carried it on long slings from a ring set in the shoulder belt, so that the chape clattered over the cobbles.

Sergeants of battalion companies, grenadier companies, fusiliers and light infantry carried swords, the last-named in addition to the musket, bayonet and cartridge pouch. These NCO swords were probably of special pattern, in some cases of regimental patterns; but no actual specimens have been traced. The 1st and 3rd Foot Guards certainly carried special-pattern weapons, of which examples survive.

Pistols

It is known that many officers of German units fighting in the Peninsula carried flintlock pistols in belted holsters. There are several mentions of British officers carrying pistols, but no direct evidence of their using holsters has been traced. Since some method of carrying these cumbersome weapons must have been adopted, the use of holsters seems logical; they were not unknown in the British Army, since we have the example of the holstered pistols of Royal Horse Artillery Rocket Troop personnel. Another practical solution, much seen in the navies of the day, was the use of a flat brass or iron 'belt hook' on the side of the pistol, fixed near the breech and lying parallel to the barrel.

Apart from heavy cavalry horse pistols, lighter weapons of private acquisition were probably quite common. Usually purchased in pairs, they had barrels between eight and ten inches long, of 20 or 24 bore, and locks fitted with sliding safety bolts behind the cocks, which could be fixed at half-cock. These pistols were used extensively by naval officers.

Ammunition

Charges for muskets were prepared in cartridges. A waxed or greased paper tube was rolled up around a powder charge sufficient for priming and firing, and a .753 calibre lead ball; the cartridge paper was cut to a regulation size and rolled with the aid of a wooden former. The powder end of the tube was tightly folded and bent over, to prevent spillage; the ball was at the other end, 'tied off' with a thread round the outside of the paper. The folded end was torn off with the teeth when the cartridge was used.

The Cartridge Pouch

Cartridges were usually issued in tied bundles of ten; the soldier untied these and inserted them in his pouch. This was of black leather; for the Foot Guards alone it was fitted with two small straps and buckles for attachment to the crossbelt, but the normal pattern had loops on its rear face and buckles on its bottom surface to accept the tapered, pierced ends of the crossbelt. For regiments of Foot the flap was plain, but the Foot Guards had

Hamilton Smith's plate of the drum major, a pioneer, a drummer and a fifer of a regiment of Foot, 1812. Note the drum major's officer's-pattern jacket with silver lace; and the bearskin caps and heavily-laced coats of the drummer and fifer. These three all wear coats in reversed colours, in this case green faced with red. The pioneer—note shoulder wings with tufted edging— has a special squat bearskin cap with a brass plate bearing a crossed saw and axe or hammer. His apron is tucked up at one side, and he has a black carrying case for his felling axe slung on the left hip.

Caricature of the 'Old Buffs' (3rd Foot) on the march, by Rowlandson; it underlines some of the rigours of campaigning. Note the 'mosquito' trousers, the camp kettle and trivet slung from a musket, the soldiers carrying their women over the stream—and the dandyish officer on the right being carried by a woman. There is a record of the Duke of Wellington coming upon officers making their men carry them over a river, and ordering the soldiers to drop them on the spot! (Author's collection)

brass stamped badges: Crown and Garter for the 1st, Garter Star for the Coldstreams, and Thistle Star for the 3rd. The pouch was fitted with a tin or wooden box split honeycomb-fashion into small rectangular sections into which the separate cartridges were inserted: 36 seems to have been the normal number. The pouch flap, rounded at the corners, had a pocket of thin leather on its inner face for spare flints, turnscrew and worm.

In the field an additional 24 cartridges could be carried in a 'magazine', a tin case covered in black leather carried 'on buff belts and buckles'. They were only carried on marches when it was considered that extra ammunition might be required at short notice, but no drawing or print has been traced which shows their appearance or the precise method of attaching them to the belts —though see below.

The Belts

For the Foot Guards the pouch belt was $2\frac{1}{2}$ins. wide and the bayonet belt $2\frac{1}{4}$ins. wide; the difference was significant enough to draw adverse comments from an inspecting officer, who was displeased by the 'wide and narrow belts'. Generally infantry wore belts $2\frac{1}{8}$ins. wide, the pouch belt being fitted with buckles so as to 'admit of being shortened and lengthened'. The regimental 'breast plate' was worn on the bayonet belt, placed where the two shoulder belts crossed on the breast. On the bayonet belt were two brass D-rings to which the magazine could be attached, but the details are unclear. Besides buckles attached to the rear of the pouch, the Foot Guards had two additional brass buckles and brass tips on the pouch belt itself, giving their belts a distinctive appearance. These buckles sat about 6ins. above the pouch, but are absent in many contemporary prints of infantry of the Line.

Officers of centre companies and most grenadier companies carried their swords on shoulder belts which were fastened with a tongue-and-pin buckle concealed by the regimental breast plate. The lower end of the belt was fashioned into a tri-

Martinique, 1793:
1. Private, Grenadier Coy., 45th (Nottinghamshire) Regt.
2. Sergeant, Light Infantry, 48th (Northamptonshire) Regt.
3. Officer, 9th (East Norfolk) Regt.

A

Holland, 1793–94:

1. Private, 14th (Bedfordshire) Regt.
2. Private, Light Infantry, 1st Bn., 2nd Foot Guards
3. Officer, Light Infantry, 1st Foot Guards

B

Cape of Good Hope, 1795:
1. Private, 61st (South Gloucestershire) Regt.
2. Officer, 81st Regt.
3. Sergeant, 91st (Argyllshire Highlanders) Regt.

C

Egypt, 1801:
1. Officer, 28th (North Gloucestershire) Regt.
2. Corporal, De Roll's Swiss Infantry Regt.
3. Private, 10th (North Lincoln) Regt.

D

Corunna, 1809:
1. Private, 1st Bn., 50th (West Kent) Regt.
2. Officer, 36th (Herefordshire) Regt.
3. Sergeant, 1st Bn., 26th (Cameronians) Regt.

E

Walcheren, 1809:
1. Officer, 2nd Bn., 8th (The King's) Regt.
2. Ensign, 1st Bn., 36th (Herefordshire) Regt.
3. Sergeant major, 1st Bn., 32nd (Cornwall) Regt.
4. Corporal, Grenadier Coy.,
   1st Bn., 6th (1st Warwickshire) Regt.

F

Salamanca, 1812:
1.   Corporal, 1st Bn., 48th (Northamptonshire) Regt.
2.   Officer, Light Infantry, 1st Bn., 30th (Cambridgeshire) Regt.
3.   Drummer, 3rd Bn., 27th (Enniskillen) Regt.

G

Waterloo, 1815:
1. Sergeant major, 33rd (1st Yorkshire, West Riding) Regt.
2. Private, 69th (South Lincolnshire) Regt.
3. Adjutant, 54th (West Norfolk) Regt.

angular leather gusset which was pierced to provide a frog for the sword. Officers of light infantry companies and regiments carried their sharply curved swords on slings from a large ring attached to the lower end of their shoulder belts. Mounted officers and field-rank officers used waistbelts and swords suspended from slings.

Officers and senior NCOs of the light infantry companies and regiments carried whistles suspended on chains on the fronts of their shoulder belts.

Soldiers and NCOs armed with muskets carried a steel 'picker' and a small brush on leather laces or fine chains, looped on to a breast button of the jacket and around the shoulder belts. These were essential tools; even though soldiers were not encouraged to dismantle the locks of their muskets —that was the job of the armourer—they had to keep the lock and vent clean, which required constant attention when on campaign. A dozen shots were enough to cause massive fouling of the inside and outside of the whole area of the lock, clogging the vent hole from the priming pan, and coating as much as a foot-long area of the outside of the weapon with a grey deposit of burned powder. (The turnscrew stowed inside the pouch lid was also in constant use, to loosen the jaws of the cock and adjust the position of the flint; few flints were still properly serviceable after more than a dozen or so shots.)

Haversacks and Canteens

Rations—often enough for three days at a time— were carried in a canvas or coarse linen bag slung on a broad belt of the same material over the right shoulder. The deep flap was fastened by two buttons. Hamilton Smith's plate of the Foot Guards shows black haversacks; other prints show pale, neutral shades of off-white or fawn.

The standard British canteen, sometimes termed the 'Italian' canteen, was a small, flattened wooden barrel bound with iron and carried on a blackened leather strap. It weighed about 3lbs. and was carried on the left hip on top of the haversack. Sergeants, whose swords hung on the left, are often illustrated with haversack and canteen on the right hip. The canteen strap passed through iron brackets riveted to the edge of the barrel, which had a metal neck and a cork secured

by a cord. The outer face of the canteen could be painted, chiselled or burnt with some regimental and/or company identification, and sometimes with the broad arrow. Illustrations show canteens painted overall in a light blue colour. Hamilton Smith shows a different pattern carried by Foot Guards. Officers carried either the 'ammunition' pattern or privately purchased types such as metal flasks, or soda water bottles in wicker or leather carriers.

Knapsacks

From the 1790s to 1805 the infantryman wore a knapsack which had been in use since the days of the American Revolution; this was a soft canvas pack which closed rather like an envelope. In 1805 a new design was accepted, manufactured by the firm of Trotter situated in Soho Square. This was of black laquered canvas reinforced with leather at the corners, and fastened rather in the style of a suitcase. It was given a rigid appearance, even

Hamilton Smith's plate of an officer of Foot in winter clothing, 1812; the 'Belgic' shako is already shown, but was not a general issue by this date—Hamilton Smith was extremely up-to-date in his details, on at least one occasion illustrating a headgear which was under discussion but was never actually issued. Note the high collar of the greatcoat; folded down, it would reveal the facing colour of the jacket collar. The officer wears the gorget and carries the straight sword, and has tied his crimson sash over the coat; note the white lining showing at the front corner. The cape was only attached to the grey coat at the base of the collar, allowing equipment belts to be worn over the coat but under the cape, and even giving some protection to the top of the knapsack— see the soldier in the right background, whose coat is unbuttoned to reveal the laced jacket.

when empty, by the fitting of rectangles of wood inside the top, bottom and side surfaces. This may have been smart and soldierly in appearance, but it was extremely uncomfortable; the edges of the boards pressed into the spine, and the horizontal strap which buckled across the chest, uniting the two shoulder straps, caused serious constriction of the lungs. There are many medical records of the serious injury to health caused by Trotter's infamous knapsack, especially among heavily laden soldiers on punishing marches. Both folding and box types continued in use together during the Napoleonic Wars; there are records of militiamen newly mustered into Line units for the 1815 campaign still wearing the old type. Regimental numbers or devices were often painted on the rear, exposed face of the pack, sometimes on a background of facing colour.

Movements and Drill

The March

Reveille was normally one and a half hours before daybreak. Assembly was beaten by drum or sounded by bugle, and men were ordered to form on the Camp Colour NCOs by companies.[1] Columns had to be ready to march by daylight.

Orders were issued by the Brigade Major. NCOs were ordered to see that the men were properly dressed and had their correct accoutrements. Subalterns were ordered to visit the companies to make sure the NCOs were doing their duties properly. Staff sergeants had to ensure that baggage was packed. Outlying piquets returned to their companies. Where possible the Commissary, with butchers, were sent on ahead with an officer responsible for reporting to the Assistant Quartermaster General at the next station, where he was informed of billeting and quartering arrangements, and the meat was prepared for the arrival of the men.

A Division mustering for the march in such a manner, involving the assembly and preparation of some 6,000 men plus hundreds of animals,

needed at least an hour for the men to dress, accoutre, roll blankets, form in squads, be paraded in companies, be sized, 'told off', and marched to their position on the assembly point. Before the march commenced firelocks were inspected, flints checked, locks tested, and the weapons were often fired into the air to check that the barrels were clear. Once the march was under way the Provost Marshal and his assistants circulated the camp area to chase out stragglers. The baggage train with the officers' bat-horses and servants followed the column, with the mule teams carrying reserve ammunition and biscuit. Behind them came the battalion womenfolk, the sutlers, and other camp followers. The Provost Marshal brought up the rear.

All officers had to remain in their stations during the march. Majors marched in the rear of their respective 'wings' of the battalion; if there was only one major he marched at the rear of the battalion column. Captains marched in the rear of their companies. Commanding officers and adjutants moved up and down the column ensuring that all was well. Attached officers such as Engineers marched at the head of the infantry of the Division.

As the men moved out of camp or quarters they marched at attention and in silence, until the order 'March at Ease'. The ranks were then opened and the files were loosened. Men were only allowed to quit the ranks if they were ill or if they needed to relieve themselves. Before doing so they had to obtain a ticket or certificate from the Orderly Sergeant on approval of their company commander. The tickets were returned to the orderly sergeant when the men rejoined their company; the NCO kept a list of those to whom tickets had been given. The Provost staff at the rear of the column examined the tickets of stragglers to make sure they had permission to fall out; in theory a man who dropped out without a ticket was brought before a court martial, but in severe situations such as the retreat on Corunna these formalities were probably widely ignored.

Half an hour after moving off the column halted for breakfast; thereafter it halted at regular intervals to give the men a chance to rest and relieve themselves, arms being carefully piled first. On long, arduous marches provision was made for

[1] These NCOs carried flags 18ins. square in the regimental facing colour, bearing the regimental number. The poles were 7ft. 6ins. long.

the replacement of badly worn shoes. In the Peninsula local sandals were provided, but they were apparently disliked for their generally poor quality. On some marches such shoes could be issued in the morning and worn out by nightfall.

Basic Drill

A detailed review of the field exercises and movements on parade is obviously not possible here. The following précis is intended to give a general picture of how the infantryman stood, marched and manoeuvred.

Standing in the Ranks

The soldier was instructed to stand square, head and eyes to the front, and only to turn the eyes to the 'point of dressing'.

The order 'March'

The first step was with the left foot. The feet were never stamped, and the first step had to be the same regulation length as any other. When soldiers moved they had to dress by the 'pivot flank' if in column, or by the head of the file when filing. When the battalion marched in line, dressing was by the Colours.

The order 'Halt'

The foot in the air had to finish its step, and the other was brought down without stamping. When 'Dress' was given, eyes turned to the pivot flank, where the platoon commander stood and corrected the line.

In Line

When marching in line the men were instructed to keep the shoulders level. They had to be able just to touch their neighbours, and the rear ranks were always ordered to 'keep locked up'.

In Column

The ranks were one pace apart. Arms were only allowed to be carried at the 'Support' position in the crook of the elbow when the battalion was halted or moving in column. When marching in line or wheeling, forming into line or dressing, they were carried 'Shouldered'.

Battalion halted to fire a volley

Sergeants fell back to ensure the rear rank kept 'well locked up'. When the battalion manoeuvred in sub-divisions officers took post in front of platoons and sergeants marched to the pivots of the leading sub-division.

Officer and Colour Sergeant of the 9th (East Norfolk) Regiment, 1812. The regiment's special 'Britannia' badge, awarded in February 1800, and partly seen on the furled Colour, is also shown on the officer's shako plate and the NCO's belt plate; note also the 'IX' beneath it on the Colour. The Colour is partly furled for ease of handling in action; and the officer is covered by the sergeant's pike. He wears grey breeches and Hessian boots, and his sash is tied over the sword belt and the bandolier supporting the flag staff 'bucket'.

Pioneers

In column they marched in front of the battalion; in line they were formed two deep, nine paces to the rear of the rear rank, in the centre of the line.

Drummers

In column, or close column, the drummers were always with their companies but on the flank. In line the grenadier and light company drummers were six paces to the rear of their respective companies. Battalion company drummers were separated in two divisions and formed six paces behind the 3rd and 7th Companies. When the battalion was in open rank they kept a six-pace interval from the rear rank.

The Band of Music

In column of march it was posted on the flank of the column. In line it was posted in a single rank behind the centre of the battalion, 12 paces behind the rear rank. On parade, when the battalion was in open order, it was placed between the Colours in the front rank.

Troops at drill—Atkinson's view shows the drill sergeant with his cane, demonstrating the 'point toe' march. Recruits wear the shako and white long-sleeved waistcoat with duck trousers. Just visible above the hind quarters of the field officer's horse is the rear view of a drummer's head, with clubbed hair. (Author's collection)

An unusual Hamilton Smith plate showing a grenadier and a light infantryman of the 29th (Worcestershire) Regiment of Foot in full dress of c.1812—white breeches and long black gaiters. Grenadiers did not wear the bearskin cap on campaign. The regimental lace, with blue and yellow lines in the white tape, is shown here in pairs with pointed ends; De Bosset (1803) lists paired loops with squared ends. Note that the light company man holds his equipment belts down with a practical waistbelt; we have records of troops in action using the musket sling in this way. The grenadier's old-style folding pack bears the regimental number in a wreath below a scroll.

Camp Colour Men

Once the battalion was moving the commanding officer directed two Camp Colour NCOs to the rear of each flank; they had to run out to give points of march, forming, wheeling and dressing.

To Stand at Ease

On the command the right foot was drawn back about six inches and the weight of the body was brought upon it; the left knee was slightly bent; the hands were brought together in front of the body; the shoulders were kept back and square; the head faced the front, but the whole attitude was 'without constraint'.

Attention

Hands had to fall smartly down the outside of the thighs; the right heel was brought in line with the left and the soldier resumed 'a proper attentive position'.

The Marching Step

The pace was 30ins., and recruits were instructed to take 75 steps per minute.

The Quick March

The pace was unchanged, but there were 108 to the minute. This pace was used during the filing of divisions into line, into column, or from column into line, and by battalions manoeuvring as columns. It was occasionally used by small bodies of men in column of march when there were no obstacles, but was not used by large bodies of men in movement, on account of fatigue.

Wheeling Time

The length of step was reduced to 20ins., and there were 120 paces per minute. This step was primarily for the purpose of wheeling; the outer files had to lengthen pace to 33ins.

Marking Time

'The cadence was continued without gaining ground'. The foot which was advancing when the order was given completed the step, and the feet were then thrown out alternately and brought back square with each other until the command 'Ordinary step', when the usual 30in. pace was resumed.

The Plummet

An instrument used to measure the rate of march, carried by the Drill Sergeant of every squad. They were of several lengths, being musket balls suspended on strings marked off to give the correct pace when the ball was swung: 75 steps = 24ins.,

108 steps = 12ins., and 120 steps = 10ins., in round figures.

Parade Ground Marked Off

A section of the parade ground was marked off and painted with the correct length of pace. Recruits practised on this until they could make the step automatically, perfectly, and without thought.

Marching

The soldier did not swing his arms as he marched. He drilled with the arm and fingers extended and the hand firmly down beside the thigh. The toe was pointed when marching, and always kept near the ground except when marking time, 'gliding' rather than stepping. Drill Sergeants kept watch to see if they could see the soles of the shoes, which meant the recruit was marching incorrectly; the feet had to be placed flat on the ground and not 'heel and toe'.

Falling In

The platoon fell in for drill in three ranks, in close order, with shouldered firelocks, files lightly touching but not crowded. Each man occupied a space of about 22ins. The commander of the post was on the right of the front rank, covered by his sergeant in the rear rank. Two other sergeants formed a fourth or 'supernumerary' rank three paces in the rear. The platoon was then 'told off' in sub-divisions and, if of sufficient strength, into four sections. A section was not less than five files, but it often happened that for drill purposes only three sections could be mustered. The four best-trained men were placed in the front rank on the right and left of each sub-division.

Forming Square

The classic protection for infantry against attack by cavalry. The battalions were drilled to form square from either line or column, the relative position of the companies differing in accordance with the original formation. This complicated manoeuvre had to be carried out swiftly, calmly, and without impediment. Once the four sides of the square were closed up, either two or four deep, with the field officers, drums and Colours in the centre, it was in most circumstances almost impregnable. However, if the manoeuvre was badly executed and one face became broken or disarrayed, allowing the enemy to break into the centre, the result could be catastrophic; this movement was therefore practised endlessly, until the men could perform it in under a minute and without thought. The confidence of steady infantry in this formation is perhaps indicated by the famous occasion at Quatre Bras when a Highland regiment formed square while under cavalry attack and actually trapped some French lancers inside, dispatching them in short order and apparently without endangering the integrity of the square.

Regimental Distinctions

A more complete breakdown of regimental identities will appear in the next volume. The following list is a basic guide to regimental facing colours, the colour of officers' lace and buttons, and the shape and spacing of soldiers' lace

Officers of the 12th (East Suffolk) Regiment, 1815; note the green feather tuft, shoulder wings and whip-sash of the light company officer, and the single epaulette of the battalion company officer. The former carries his slung, curved sword; the latter has a straight sword frogged at the hip, and grenade decorations on his turnbacks. (Author's collection)

2nd Foot Guards, 1792. The large bicorne is worn over the right eye so as not to foul the shouldered musket; it has a dark feather and white stay-cords. Note white breeches and black gaiters. (Author's collection)

sources. Sergeants wore plain white lace. Royal Marines had plain white lace down the front of their jackets. Foot Guards had white lace down the front of the jackets and around the top edge of the cuffs, unlike Line regiments: and their sergeants wore gold lace.

Regiment	Facings	Lace/ 'Metal'	Men's Lace
1st Foot Guards	Blue	G	B1
2nd Foot Guards	Blue	G	P2
3rd Foot Guards	Blue	G	P3
1st Foot	Blue	G	S2
2nd	Blue	S	S1
3rd	Buff	S	S2
4th	Blue	S	B1
5th	Yellowish Green	S	B1
6th	Deep Yellow	S	S2
7th	Blue	G	S1
8th	Blue	G	S1
9th	Pale Yellow	S	S2
10th	Pale Yellow	S	S1
11th	Blue-green	G	B2
12th	Pale Yellow	G	B2
13th	Yellow	S	S2
14th	Buff	S	S2
15th	Yellow	S	S2
16th	Yellow	S	S1
17th	White	S	S2
18th	Blue	G	S2
19th	Blue-green	G	S2
20th	Pale Yellow	S	S2
21st	Blue	G	S2
22nd	Buff	G	B2
23rd	Blue	G	B1
24th	Blue-green	S	S2
25th	Deep Yellow	G	B1
26th	Pale Yellow	S	S2
27th	Pale Buff	G	S1
28th	Yellow	S	S2
29th	Yellow	S	S2
30th	Pale Yellow	S	B1
31st	Buff	S	S1
32nd	White	G	S2
33rd	Red	S	B2
34th	Yellow	S	S2
35th	Orange	S	S2
36th	Yellowish Green	G	S2
37th	Yellow	S	S2
38th	Yellow	S	B1
39th	Light Green	G	S2
40th	Deep Buff	G	S1
41st	Red	S	B1
42nd	Blue	G	B1

buttonhole loops, from the diagrams of C. Phillipe De Bosset, published in 1803. Since these distinctions do not apply to the uniform of the Rifle battalions of the 60th, or the 95th Rifles, they are not included.

The abbreviations are as follows: G = gold, S = silver. S = Square-ended loops; B = Bastion-formed loops; P = Pointed loops. Loop spacing was either single, i.e. equidistant loops; in pairs; or in sets of three. This is indicated here e.g. 'B2' = Bastion loops, in pairs; 'S1' = Square-ended loops, single spaced.

The men's lace was white tape with interwoven lengthways lines or 'worms' of different regimental colours and combinations; these are not listed here, as many contradictions exist in surviving

43rd	White	S	S2		De Roll's	Sky Blue	S	S1
44th	Yellow	S	S1		De Meuron's	Sky Blue	S	B1
45th	Blue-green	S	B2		Queen's Germans	Pale Yellow	S	S1
46th	Pale Yellow	S	S2		De Watteville's	Black	S	B1
47th	White	S	S2		*West India Regiments*			
48th	Buff	G	S2		1st	White	S	S1
49th	Blue-green	G	B1		2nd	Deep Yellow	G	S1
50th	Black	G	S2		3rd	Deep Yellow	S	S1
51st	Blue-green	G	S2		4th	Deep Yellow	S	S1
52nd	Buff	S	S2		5th	Blue-green	S	S1
53rd	Red	G	S2		6th	Deep Yellow	S	S1
54th	Yellow-green	S	S2		Garrison			
55th	Blue-green	G	S2		Battalions	Blue	G	S2
56th	Purple	S	S2		Royal Marines	Blue	G	S2
57th	Pale Yellow	G	S2					
58th	Black	G	S1					
59th	White	G	B1					
60th	Blue	S	S2					
61st	Buff	S	S1					
62nd	Buff	S	S2					
63rd	Blue-green	S	S2					
64th	Black	G	S2					
65th	White	G	S2					
66th	Yellow-green	S	S1					
67th	Pale Yellow	S	S2					
68th	Blue-green	S	S2					
69th	Blue-green	G	S2					
70th	Black	G	S1					
71st	Buff	S	S1					
72nd	Deep Yellow	S	B1					
73rd	Blue-green	G	B1					
74th	White	G	S1					
75th	Yellow	S	S2					
76th	Red	S	S2					
77th	Yellow	S	S1					
78th	Buff	G	B1					
79th	Blue-green	G	S2					
80th	Yellow	G	S2					
81st	Buff	S	S2					
82nd	Pale Yellow	S	B2					
83rd	Pale Yellow	G	S2					
84th	Pale Yellow	S	S2					
85th	Yellow	S	S2					
86th	Yellow	S	S2					
87th	Blue-green	G	S2					
88th	Yellow	S	S2					
89th	Black	G	S2					
90th	Deep Buff	G	S2					
91st	Pale Yellow	S	S2					
93rd	Yellow	S	S2					
94th	Blue-green	G	S2					
96th	Buff	S	S2					
New South Wales Regt.	Yellow	S	S2					
Staff Corps	Blue	S	-					

Officer, 2nd Foot Guards, 1792. The large bicorne hat has no feather tuft, but large tasselled 'pulls' at the corners. The coat has long lapels and full turned-back skirts; note the particular design of the epaulette, recalling the shoulder-knot of cord from which this item evolved. The hair is in a loose, powdered style. The sash is worn over the waistcoat but beneath the coat. (Author's collection)

Detail from a contemporary painting of a battle scene, 1812, showing British infantry wearing white pantaloons. (Wallis & Wallis)

Officer's shako, 1812 pattern; an excellent example showing the universal pattern plate and a large cut-feather plume. (Wallis & Wallis)

The Plates

A: Martinique, 1793
A1: Private, Grenadier Company, 45th (Nottinghamshire) Regiment
A2: Sergeant, Light Infantry, 48th (Northamptonshire) Regiment
A3: Officer, 9th (East Norfolk) Regiment

In 1793 the battalion companies of the 21st and the massed flank companies of the 9th, 15th, 21st, 45th, 48th, 3/60th and 67th Regiments were on the island of Martinique. The system of massing flank companies, used to considerable purpose during the American War of Independence, was continued into 1794. In that year the grenadiers and light infantry of the 13th, 20th and 49th Regiments under the command of Majors Brent Spencer and Coote-Manningham (later to command the 95th Rifles) were in action on St Domingo, presently reinforced by the 22nd, 23rd and 41st. In 1794 a much larger force was assembled on Martinique under Sir Charles Grey, who formed three brigades comprising the 15th, 39th and 43rd; the 56th, 63rd and 64th; and the 6th, 58th and 70th. The principle of massing flank companies continued with grenadiers formed into three battalions under Colonel Campbell: the 6th, 8th, 12th, 17th, 22nd, 23rd, 31st, 41st and 56th; the 9th 33rd, 34th, 38th, 40th and 58th; and the 15th, 21st, 39th, 43rd, 55th, 60th, 64th and 70th.

The campaigns on the islands were rigorous, and the expeditionary force was much weakened by malaria and yellow fever, so much so that in the end it was defeated by disease rather than by the French.

Most troops wore the 'round' hat, either the black type with or without a fur crest, or a lightweight white hat manufactured of straw or cane, with linen covers and muslin curtains which could be soaked in water to keep the head cool, or let down to protect the neck. The heavy, lined red coat was discarded in favour of a loose-fitting jacket made to button across the body. There has been research and speculation as to its appearance, and whether or not it was decorated with lace. I have chosen to show it (A1) with lace, as this follows the logical development of the British style of infantry uniform during the last half of the 18th century. The legs and stomach were protected by close-fitting, one-piece 'mosquito' trousers, fashioned to shape over the shoes.

Nevertheless, the effect of marching in steamy swamp-jungles reduced clothing to shreds, and it was reported that many units were literally dressed in rags, and often barefoot. As a consequence, locally and no doubt crudely made clothing was taken into use. The sergeant wears only the white, sleeved waistcoat; his rank is indicated by the sash with a central stripe of regimental facing colour, and by the epaulettes—I have elected to show these in yellow worsted, following the precedent that only sergeant majors and quartermaster sergeants wore gold or silver at this date.

B: Holland, 1793–94
B1: Private, 14th (Bedfordshire) Regiment
B2: Private, Light Infantry, 1st Bn., 2nd Foot Guards
B3: Officer, Light Infantry, 1st Foot Guards

In 1793 three battalions of Foot Guards commanded by Col. Gerard Lake, 1st FG, landed in Holland. By 1794 there were four battalions of Foot Guards in the Low Countries, formed from the light infantry companies of all three regiments. In addition, Abercromby commanded an infantry brigade comprising the 14th, 37th, and 53rd Regiments. By July of that year there were seven brigades of infantry under his command, namely: *1st Bde.* 3rd, 63rd and 88th; *2nd Bde.* 8th, 33rd and 44th; *3rd Bde.* 12th, 38th and 55th; *4th Bde.* 14th, 53rd and 37th; *5th Bde.* 19th, 42nd and 54th; *6th Bde.* 27th, 28th and 89th; *7th Bde.* 7th, 40th, 57th, 59th and 87th—besides the Loyal Emigrants, the York Rangers and Rohan's Regiment, giving a total of some 583 officers and 21,179 men.

The calibre of this army was severely criticised by foreign observers. They noted its bad discipline, the ineffectiveness of company commanders, the drunkenness, especially among officers, the poor quality of the colonels, and the paucity of general officers. Little effort had been made to clothe the soldiers adequately. Some raw recruits were dressed only in 'slop' jackets, without waistcoats or drawers, or even stockings. The supply system was inadequate, and hospital facilities appalling.

The weather caused considerable hardship and there was a high level of sickness, mainly miasmic fever caused by the marshy terrain. The men were constantly damp and suffered from the ague. In the absence of proper clothing issue the troops made shift with what they could find, and acquired local wide-legged trousers and civilian 'surtouts' besides clumsily repairing their own coats.

The 'round' hat was still favoured, especially by light infantry, but some units seem to have adapted their cocked hats by looping up one side and decorating the hat with feathers. There is a

Soldier's shako and jacket of the 83rd Regiment, Peninsular War period; note the depth of the shako plate in relation to the height of the cap. This dull red jacket, one of very few surviving examples of a ranker's uniform, is on display in the Musée de l'Armée, Paris; when previously in the Brunon Collection at the Musée de l'Emperi it had shoulder wings of slightly dubious provenance—note the absence of drawn thread tufting at the ends of the shoulder straps, suggesting that it probably was, in fact, a flank company jacket. Note the slanting style of the breast loops. (Author's collection)

drawing by Langendyck which shows British infantry with moustaches. The form of the Guards flank company shoulder wings is taken from a naif sketch made by a Dutchman in Ghent in 1794. At this date battalion companies wore two plain shoulder straps in facing colour with lace trim.

C: Cape of Good Hope, 1795
C1: Private, 61st (South Gloucestershire) Regiment
C2: Officer, 81st Regiment
C3: Sergeant, 91st (Argyllshire Highlanders) Regiment
In 1795 the Cape of Good Hope, South Africa, was seized from the Dutch, at that time allies of the French. It was hoped to develop the area as a naval base serving both the Indian Ocean and the South Atlantic. The expeditionary force com-

Field officer, 25th (The King's Own Borderers) Regiment of Foot, 1812. Goddard's careful print shows an officer wearing the long-skirted coatee: note heavy gold lacing on both sides of the breast; two bullion epaulettes; Mameluke-pattern sword worn on slings from a waist belt; and the scale loop on the hat. Until 1805 the breastplate of this regiment was gilt, oval, with '25' set in a Garter lettered SUSSEX REGIMENT; that worn after the change of designation was in a very elaborate, baroque style with an equally complicated slide. (Author's collection)

prised the 8th Light Dragoons, the 91st (formerly the 98th), the 61st and the 81st Regiments of Foot. A local Hottentot Corps was formed, and companies of the Royal Artillery joined the force from both Britain and India. In 1800 two 'Boy Regiments', the 22nd and 34th, arrived in the Cape; and the 65th replaced the 61st, which was bound for the Red Sea and later Egypt, with some elements of the 8th Light Dragoons. In August 1801 two companies of the 91st were withdrawn; and later that year a company of Mounted Infantry was formed from elements of the 22nd, 65th, 81st and 91st.

From the outset officers and men wore 'round' hats, which were about 6ins. high with 4in. brims. They had feathers in company colours: white-over-red, white and green for battalion, grenadier and light infantry companies, with some use of black as well. These hats were ordered for troops proceeding to warm stations. The men were also issued with the loose, buttoned-over jackets for troops in West or East Indian stations. These coats are described by L. E. Buckell as having lace loops on the breast, lace around the collar, and lace loops on the round cuffs. They appear to have been the precursors of the closed jackets which became universal for British infantry in 1797. For drills, fatigues, and on campaign up-country the troops wore white long-sleeved waistcoats, and with both jackets and waistcoats white pantaloons or trousers were worn with black gaiters. The 91st wore this same uniform, despite their Highland designation, and are recorded as wearing blue trousers on Sundays. According to John Shipp the Mounted Infantry wore green jackets with white trousers and carried rifles with browned barrels. The battalion company men now had a white drawn worsted fringe decorating the end of their shoulder straps. The buff breeches (C2) replaced white in regiments with buff facings. Different contemporary illustrations show the sergeant's sash being worn both at the waist and across the shoulder.

D: Egypt, 1801
D1: Officer, 28th (North Gloucestershire) Regiment
D2: Corporal, De Roll's Regiment of Swiss Infantry
D3: Private, 10th (North Lincoln) Regiment
In May 1800 Sir Ralph Abercromby was

appointed Commander-in-Chief of forces in the Mediterranean, including Gibraltar, and later commanded the expedition to Egypt. Two forces were involved. The first, led by Abercromby, was transported by Admiral Lord Keith's fleet, and landed at Aboukir Bay east of Alexandria on 8 March 1801. The second, led by Maj.Gen. Baird, sailed from Bombay, landing at Cosseir and marching overland to join the rest of the army.

During the battle of Alexandria the 28th Regiment, led by Col. Paget, gained renown and the right to wear the unique 'back badge' on their headdress during their back-to-back action in the attack on the left of the ruins of the Ptolemies. The 10th Regiment, together with the 80th, 86th and 88th Regiments and the 1st and 7th Bombay Native Regiments, formed part of the force from India. De Roll's Swiss were commanded by Lt.Col. Baron de Dürler.

In December 1800 the ubiquitous and cumbersome felt hat, worn in such a variety of styles throughout the entire 18th century, was discarded in favour of a leather cap called a 'shako'. The first type was a heavy headdress about 9ins. tall, 7ins. broad across the top, and with a flat 2in.-broad peak. It had a cockade of black crêpe and a large brass plate, 6ins. high by 4ins. broad. This was stamped with a universal design of the Royal Cypher set in a Garter surrounded by trophies of arms and Colours. Above the Garter was the Crown, and below it the Royal Crest. Several regiments wore ancient or special badges in place of or in addition to the Royal Crest, and some had badges in place of the Cypher. The leather was japanned. Officers continued to wear either a large cocked hat or the much-favoured 'round' hat, especially on tropical stations. The woollen tufts worn on the shakos were in company colours; officers wore large cut-feather ornaments in the same colours. Officers of light infantry companies wore shakos.

Contemporary sketches of the 61st Regiment in Egypt show all ranks in 'round' hats; some officers have a pattern with a fur crest or roach. The latter type is also shown worn by officers and some men in the panoramic painting of Seringapatam by Sir K. Porter, and there seems little doubt that some of Baird's units would also have worn this.

De Roll's comprised 20 officers and 492 NCOs

Another 1812-pattern officer's shako, showing the regimental number '56' embossed below the Royal Cypher. (Wallis & Wallis)

and men when it landed. The leading authority Vicomte Grouvel states that the officers wore 'round' hats in Egypt, and some French sources suggest that NCOs and men continued to wear black straw 'round' hats with fur crests and scarlet turbans, although some shakos were issued before they left Gibraltar. The felt illustrated (D2) is from notes in Lawson's collection describing a Swiss watercolour showing a soldier of the regiment in Egypt.

Knapsacks were ordered to be left on board ship before disembarkation, and only the blanket was carried slung across the back. The corporal's insignia of rank was still a white worsted epaulette with a small fringe, on the right shoulder only. Hair was still powdered and clubbed; in flank companies it was plaited, the plait being tucked back up under the shako. The red jacket worn by D2 is still basically the cutaway or 'roll-fronted' type described under Plate C, although this foreign regiment had certain peculiarities which should not be taken as universal; and D3 also wears this type of jacket. The fringe at the end of the shoulder strap of the battalion company men has now evolved into a worsted tuft of quite substantial proportions.

35

Heading illustration from De Bosset plate of 1803: a sergeant of a battalion company, a grenadier of Foot Guards, an artilleryman, and a soldier of a regiment of Foot. Note the sergeant's horizontal pocket flaps, the queued hair, and the envelope-style knapsack. The grenadier has a matchcase on his pouch belt. (Author's collection)

E: Corunna, 1809
E1: Private, 1st Bn., 50th (West Kent) Regiment
E2: Officer, 36th (Herefordshire) Regiment
E3: Sergeant, 1st Bn., 26th (Cameronians) Regiment
Sir John Moore commenced the retreat from Sahagun to Corunna on Christmas Day 1808, moving his men out by brigades only 36 hours before the French arrived in force. They marched in appalling weather from Sahagun to Astorga, crossing the Esla to Villafranca, Lugo, Belanzos, and finally Corunna. Two routes were chosen: Baird took the shorter link via Astorga and Hope, Fraser and Paget marched south via Benavente, while the Light Brigade struck westwards to Vigo via Ponferrado and Orense.

The horrifying retreat led through icy mountain passes and rugged gorges, covered by Paget's heroic rearguard. Discontent spread, and drunkenness became rife; some troops looted, others raped, and many were left dying on the road from privation and excesses. After Nogales the route began to present a terrible spectacle, with ragged, often barefoot soldiers and their women dropping in their tracks from sickness, hunger, and the dreadful cold. Ox-carts full of wounded and dying were abandoned by the roadside. The track was littered for mile after mile with discarded equipment and knapsacks, and the forlorn dead and dying.

In 1806 a new pattern of felt shako replaced the heavy, uncomfortable leather type. Queues had been abolished in July 1808, and the soldiers' hair was now cut close to the head and neck. The infantry jacket had now evolved to the shape it would keep for many years, cut square across the stomach with the skirt tails sloping sharply away. In 1802 the epaulettes and shoulder knots of sergeants and corporals were discontinued, and chevron rank distinctions were introduced. Sergeant majors and staff sergeants wore four silver bars; sergeants, three of plain white silk; and corporals, two, of regimental pattern lace. In some regiments the colonel awarded aspiring NCOs or 'chosen men' a single chevron. Chevrons were placed above the right elbow, on a backing of regimental facing colour; but there was little uniformity, some regiments wearing them point down and others point up. In 1801 the caped greatcoat was generally issued; formerly 'watch-coats' had only been issued for guard and piquet duties. In 1808 sergeants were ordered to fix collars and cuffs of the regimental facing colour, and their rank chevrons, to these coats.

F: Walcheren, 1809
F1: Officer, 2nd Bn., 8th (The King's) Regiment
F2: Ensign 1st Bn., 36th (Herefordshire) regiment
F3: Sergeant major, 1st Bn., 32nd (Cornwall) Regiment
F4: Corporal, Grenadier Company, 1st Bn., 6th (1st Warwickshire) Regiment
A British expedition consisting of 264 warships, 352 transports and 39,000 troops commanded by Lord Chatham, with Sir Eyre Coote as second in command, landed at Flushing; the town was invested on 16 August 1809. The 33,000 infantry were deployed in five divisions totalling 14 brigades. Battalions varied in strength: some barely exceeded 400 while others reached 1,000. The two battalions of Foot Guards present totalled 2,400 officers and men.

Walcheren lies in the Schelde estuary and is extremely low-lying; yet little had been learnt since 1794. By the autumn the army had an epidemic of miasmic fever, and losses eventually became so severe that the area had to be evacuated by the end of the year. Many of the troops were inadequately dressed, without blankets or flannel underclothes, and overcoats were thin.

Three battalions, including the 28th, were selected to wear experimental pantaloons or loose trousers. The 28th wore grey trousers, which proved the most successful, being virtually undamaged when they returned to the United Kingdom. Troops wearing breeches and gaiters rapidly acquired local replacements, including bargees' trousers reinforced with canvas or leather.

Greatcoats were buckled on to the knapsacks. Inside the knapsack the soldier carried two pairs of shoes, one pair of gaiters, two pairs of stockings, four brushes, a button-stick, a comb, pipeclay for whitening his belts, pen and ink, a 'slop' jacket and a fatigue cap—though the latter was often buckled beneath the cartridge pouch. If haversacks were not available the knapsack also accommodated three days' bread and two days' beef.

Sergeant majors wore double-breasted coats like those of the officers, normally with the top few inches folded open to reveal the coloured facings. They had silver lace, epaulettes and chevrons, wore sergeants' sashes and carried canes.

In March 1809 officers were ordered to wear the following badges on the epaulette straps, in the opposite metal—that is, gold in silver-laced regiments, and silver in gold-laced regiments: colonel—crown and star; lieutenant-colonel—crown; major—star; company officers of grenadiers—grenade; company officers of light infantry—bugle horn. Captains of flank companies with brevet rank wore two epaulettes over two wings. Company officers of flank companies wore wings only. Field officers wore two epaulettes, and captains one on the right shoulder, in each case with a bullion twist fringe. The subalterns wore a single right epaulette with a thin wire fringe. Adjutants wore a fringed subaltern's epaulette on the right and a fringeless epaulette on the left.

G: Salamanca, 1812

G1: Corporal, 1st Bn., 48th (Northamptonshire) Regiment

G2: Officer, Light Infantry, 1st Bn., 30th (Cambridgeshire) Regiment

G3: Drummer, 3rd Bn., 27th (Enniskillen) Regiment

Salamanca, on 22 July 1812, is considered one of Wellington's classic victories, the more impressive

Superb example of an 1812-pattern officer's shako bearing the unique plate of the 23rd (Royal Welsh Fusileers) Regiment. Below a scroll MINDEN are three devices: the Royal Cypher in a Garter; the Prince of Wales's Plumes in a Garter lettered with the regimental title; and the Sphinx above EGYPT, and an embossed XXIII. (Wallis & Wallis)

Officer, 2nd Foot Guards, c.1812, showing the laced collar lapels, and jacket front of this regiment, and the regimental belt plate; cap plates bore the same design. (Wallis & Wallis)

for being an example of instant manoeuvre to exploit aggressively a momentary enemy weakness, since Wellington's name is usually associated with impeccably sited and conducted defences rather than lightning attacks. On that day, after several weeks of marching and countermarching in fairly close contact with the Anglo-Allied army, Marshal Marmont was deploying with the intention of getting astride Wellington's line of retreat; in the course of the morning, with his view of Wellington's forces partly obscured by rolling ground, Marmont contrived to get his army dangerously stretched right across Wellington's front, with his right and left flanks drifting apart. Seizing the opportunity, Wellington executed manoeuvres of brilliant simplicity, attacking the enemy at several points simultaneously and routing them in 40 minutes; Marmont lost an arm, and 13,000 officers and men and many guns were captured. The victory led directly to the fall of Madrid to the Allies on 12 August.

In June 1811 a report stated that the existing shako was unsatisfactory because of its easily damaged form, unsteadiness on the head, ineffectiveness as protection against sword cuts, and lack of protection against bad weather. As a result a new pattern was designed and submitted to the Board, but was not finally approved until 1812; it is unlikely in the extreme that any unit at Salamanca would have worn it, indeed its use at any time in the Peninsula remains in doubt, bearing in mind the uncertainty of the supply system.

However, by 1812 the use of trousers by British infantry, except for full dress, had become universal. The grey-blue type were used in cool weather, and white trousers of linen or duck were substituted in the very hot, dry Spanish summers. Replacement of uniform clothing was erratic, and many items had to be made up from locally-procured homespun, which was usually brown. It was used to repair jackets, and sometimes to make up complete replacement coats and trousers.

The officer (G2) wears one of several known combinations of light company insignia on his shako. Red cloth wings, edged and fringed silver, bear gold bugle horn company badges on ornate backings; exact details of the design and proportions of such items as wings and epaulettes tended to vary from officer to officer. Bugle horns

also decorate the short turn backs of the jacket which is worn here with the lapels buttoned fully open. It is more normal in portraits to see only the top corners opened to expose two small triangles of facings. Note the light infantry whip-sash, and the curved sabre on slings. In the background is a Camp Colour NCO.

Up until 1812 drummers wore reversed clothing, i.e. the jackets were the colour of the facing with red collars, cuffs, shoulder straps, wings and turnbacks, all decorated with regimental lace. Drummers of 'red-faced' regiments wore white coats faced with red, and those of Royal regiments red faced with blue. The drums were of wood, the fronts being painted in the facing colour, with badges or the Royal Cypher and the number of the regiment; in this case, the famous castle badge of the 27th.

H: Waterloo, 1815
H1: Sergeant major, 33rd (1st Yorkshire, West Riding) Regiment
H2: Private, 69th (South Lincolnshire) Regiment
H3: Adjutant, 54th (West Norfolk) Regiment

In March 1815 the new pattern of headdress was approved, and was gradually being issued for wear by all ranks. Basically identical in shape to the Portuguese infantry's *barretina*, it is generally termed the 'Belgic' or 'Waterloo' shako. It was of felt for the rank and file, coarse beaver for sergeants, and fine beaver bound with silk for staff sergeants and officers. The cords were mixed gold and crimson for officers; white for NCOs and men of battalion and grenadier companies; and green for light infantry companies. Cap plates were copper gilt for officers and brass for NCOs and men, usually decorated with the Crown and Cypher above the regimental number—although many examples of un-numbered plates are known. Some units had extravagantly decorated plates; the Foot Guards had special Star plates, and their light infantry companies wore a bugle horn either incorporated into the plate design or worn separately above it. Light companies of Line regiments seem often to have worn regimental numbers below a bugle horn, in brass and white metal respectively, in place of the plate. The cockade was black, either of pleated silk or of coiled cord; the central button might be of regimental pattern, or charged with a grenade or bugle horn in flank companies. Officers' and staff sergeants' tufts were of cut feathers in white-over-red, white or green for battalion, grenadier or light companies; NCOs and men wore woollen tufts of the same colours. Drummers seem to have worn red-over-white tufts.

Dennis Dighton shows Foot Guards in shakos covered with black oilskin and with chin tapes or straps. Horace Vernet shows a private with an uncovered shako with a chin strap. Capt. Cadell, 28th Foot, was painted with his regiment's special 'stovepipe' shako of 1806 pattern with what appears to be a chin strap or ribbon passing up the side—presumably tying on top of the crown.

Jackets seem to have been smarter and better-fitting by 1815—a logical result of much of the Army being brought home from the Peninsula and enjoying a year of peace and parades before 'the Ogre' returned to trouble the peace of Europe once more. The cloth was dull red for rank and file, and bright scarlet for officers and senior NCOs. The regimental facing colours were still worn at collar, cuff and shoulder strap by the rank and file: the turnbacks were lined white. Buttons were of pewter for the rankers whatever the regimental lace and 'metal' colour: Foot Guards sergeants had them gilded. The loops of regimental lace set on the breast were $3\frac{1}{2}$ins. long at the neck, tapering down slightly to the waist; in some units they were set squarely on the cloth, and in others they were placed slanting upwards slightly at the outer ends. Although ten loops were the norm, some jackets had only eight; the height of the man, and the regimental loop spacing sequence, both affected this.

Flank companies still wore wings of cloth at the shoulders, red for Line regiments and blue for Foot Guards, edged with regimental lace and with darts of regimental lace across the shells. In some units the outer edge was decorated with drawn thread in a fringe or tufting of white or other colours.

Officers' jackets were double-breasted, with faced lapels and silvered or gilt buttons according to regimental 'metal'. Well tailored, and often padded to exaggerate the outline, they were of 'superfine' cloth. Some regiments were 'laced', i.e. the officers wore loops of gold or silver lace on the

breast, cuffs, rear pocket flaps and collar, as H3; others were 'non-laced', as G2, and had button holes worked only with a line of twist. H3 wears the fringeless left *contre-epaulette* of an adjutant. Note the crimson silk net sash tied at the left, holding his sword belt from flapping loosely. In some regiments officers' grey trousers had lace sidestripes; P. W. Reynolds records that the 54th had silver stripes, and the portrait of Capt. Cadell of the 28th also shows this feature.

In the background is a Colour Sergeant of the 32nd Regiment. This rank was newly instituted late in the Peninsular War for gallantry in the field. Its badge was a single chevron of regimental lace below a Union Flag below the Royal Crown, with silver swords crossed over the flag staff. It was worn on the right upper arm only.

The stripes in sergeants' sashes were supposed to be white in regiments faced red or purple, but Stadden shows red stripes for the 33rd.

Officer's shako of an unidentified Volunteer regiment, *c.*1812; the narrow peak of this unusual example is found on several other Volunteer officers' shakos of the period. The cockade is placed at the band instead of at the top, as was normal; and note the long, apparently tricolour cut feather plume. The central Crown, Garter and Cypher, surrounded here by trophies of arms and flags, are identical to the raised portion of the universal cap plate of the 'stovepipe' shako of 1800 and 1806. (Wallis & Wallis)

Notes sur les planches en couleur

A Les troupes de la Martinique portaient soit un gilet blanc à longues manches, soit une veste rouge courte décorée de parments aux couleurs du régiment avec galons en corcon. Les 'Mosquito trousers' étaient étroits, serrés autour des chaussures. Des chapeaux ronds de paille ou de canne fendue étaient portés, quelquefois avec dessus de toile, ou bien avec un couvre-nuque pour protéger contre le soleil. A cette époque, on reconnaissait les sergents aux épaulettes et à la ceinture rouge rayée aux parements du régiment; également, ils portaient une pique.

B Durant cette campagne, les couvre-chefs étaient un mélange du vieux bicorne, les bords relevés de façons différentes, et du petit chapeau rond, quelquefois porté avec de la fourrure au cimier. Le long 'coatee' était l'habit normal d'uniforme; les troupes, mal approvisionnées, acquéraient également des habits civils.

C Les chapeaux ronds avaient des houppes de laine ou de plume aux couleurs de la compagnie: blanches, blanches et rouge, et vertes pour les grenadiers, les fusiliers et l'infanterie légère respectivement. La même veste courte et le même gilet blanc utilisés à la Martinique étaient portés. Les hommes des 'battalion compagnies', c'est à dire les fusiliers, portaient alors des pattes d'épaule à franges blanches.

D Pendant l'année 1800, les shakos de cuir remplacèrent le vieux bicorne de feutre chez le simple soldat; les officiers continuèrent à porter le bicorne ou le chapeau rond. La veste courte était toujours la même qui avait été adaptée aux tropiques, avec le plastron découpé sur l'estomac. L'insigne de caporal était une épaulette blanche sur l'épaule droite. La frange aux pattes d'épaule était devenue une houppe de laine.

E En 1806 le shako de cuir fût remplacé par un modèle en feutre. La chevelure était maintenant portée courte et sans poudre. La veste du fantassin était maintenant coupée droite sur l'estomac. En 1802 l'insigne de rang des caporaux et des sergents fût changée en faveur du système désormais familier de galons en chevrons sur la manche droite. En 1809 les sergents reçurent l'ordre de porter les parements régimentaux sur les rebords de manche et le revers du col de leur capote.

F Les pantalons gris pour la campagne furent essayés pour la première fois pendant cette expédition. Les officiers portaient des vestes croisées, le plastron boutoné serré, avec seulement deux petits triangles de parements aux couleurs du régiment visibles en haut. Les sergent-majors portaient une veste du même modèle que celle des officiers.

G Les officiers des compagnies d'infanterie légère portaient des 'ailes' plutôt que des épaulettes, et une ceinture spéciale; également, des sabres courbes plutôt que droits. L'emblème en clairon était souvent porté comme badge par ces unités. Les troupes portaient des pantalons blancs, gris ou marrons pendant la campagne; blanc l'été, gris l'hiver, et en tissus marron confectionnés localement quand les fournitures normales n'étaient pas disponibles. Les tambours portaient des vestes à parement régimental, doublées de rouge, jusqu'en 1812.

H Approuvé en 1812, le nouveau shako 'Belgic' ou 'Waterloo' ne fut pas distribué de façon générale avant 1813–14, mais était porté par la plus grande part de l'infanterie en 1815. Il avait un cordon blanc de décoration pour les troupes, de cordes or et rouge tressées pour les officiers; sa forme ressemblait au modèle portugais. Des cirés étaient souvent portés en campagne. Les compagnies de grenadiers et d'infanterie légère portaient des 'ailes' aux épaules, quelquefois avec une bordure en touffe; les 'ailes' des officiers étaient rembourrées et décorées de façon élaborée, avec des dentelles ou des chaînes.

Farbtafeln

A Die Truppen in Martinique trugen entweder eine weisse langärmelige Weste oder eine kurze rote Jacke, verziert mit den Regimentsbesatzfarben und mit Litzenstreifen. Engpassende 'mosquito trousers' um die Schuhe angepasst. Runde Hüte aus Stroh oder gespaltenem Peddigrohr wurden getragen, manchmal mit einem Leinenschutz oder einer leinernen Halsklappe gegen die Sonne. Zu diesem Zeitpunkt unterschieden sich die Unteroffiziere durch die Schulterstücke und durch eine karmesinrote Schärpe mit einem Streifen in der Regimentsbesatzfarbe, und trugen eine Pike.

B In dieser Schlacht waren die Hüte eine Mischung aus dem alten bicorne, den Rand in verschiedenen Variationen aufgeschlagen, und dem kleinen runden Hut, manchmal mit einer Pelzkrone getragen. Der lange coatee war das normale Uniformkleidungsstück; die schlecht versorgten Truppen beschafften sich auch Zivilkleidung.

C Die runden Hüte trugen Büschel aus Wolle oder Federn in den Kompaniefarben: weiss, weiss und rot, und grün, gleichermassen für Grenadiere, Fusiliere und leichte Infanterie. Dieselben kurzen Jacken und weissen Westen, wie in Martinique benutzt, wurden wieder getragen. Die Männer der 'battalion companies'—z.B. Fusiliere—hatten nunmehr einen weissen Fransenbesätz am Ende ihrer Schulterklappen.

D Das Jahr 1800 sah den alten Filz-bicorne durch ein Leder-shako unter den einfachen Soldaten ersetzt; Offiziere benutzten noch den bicorne oder den runden Hut. Die kurze Jacke war noch jene, welche sich für den tropischen Gebrauch entwickelt hat, mit der Vorderseite 'weggeschnitten' über dem Bauch. Das Rangabzeichen des Korporals war eine weisses Schulterstück auf der rechten Schulter. Die Fransen an den Schulterklappen der Soldaten hatten sich nun in einen Wollbüschel verwandelt.

E Im Jahre 1806 wurde das lederne shako durch eines aus Filz ersetzt. Das Haar wurde nunmehr kurz und ungepudert getragen. Die Jacke des Infanteristen war nunmehr gerade geschnitten über dem Bauch. Im Jahre 1802 wurden die Rangabzeichen der Korporale und Unteroffiziere zu dem bekannten System der Winkel auf dem rechten Ärmel umgeändert. Im Jahre 1808 wurde den Unteroffizieren befohlen, die Regimentsbesatzfarben auf den Ärmelaufschlägen und dem Kragen ihrer Übermantel zu tragen.

F Graue Hosen zur Benutzung während des Feldzuges wurden zum ersten Mal auf dieser Expedition ausprobiert. Die Offiziere trugen doppelreihig geknöpfte Jacken, die Vorderseiten fest zugeknöpft bis auf zwei kleine Dreiecke oben, die Regimentsfarben zeigend. Sergeant-majors trugen die gleiche geformte Jacke wie die Offiziere.

G Offiziere der leichten Infanteriekompanien trugen vielmehr 'Flügel' als Schulterstücke und eine spezielle Schärpe; sie trugen gebogene Säbel anstelle von geraden Schwertern. Das Waldhornmotiv wurde von diesen Einheiten oft als Wappen getragen. Die Truppen trugen weisse, graue oder braune Hosen während eines Feldzuges; weiss im Sommer, grau im Winter und das braune örtliche Tuch, wenn die normale Ausstattung nicht zu bekommen war. Die Trommler trugen Mäntel in den Regimentsfarben, mit rot besetzt, bis zum Jahre 1812.

H Das neue 'Belgic' oder 'Waterloo' shako, für gut befunden im Jahre 1812, kam bis zum Jahre 1813–14 nicht in den allgemeinen Gebrauch, wurde jedoch im Jahre 1815 von den meisten Infanteristen getragen. Es hatte eine Kordelverzierungen für die Truppen, gold und rot gemischte Kordeln für Offiziere; seine Form sah dem portugisischen Typ ähnlich. Ölzeugschutz wurde oft während eines Feldzuges getragen. Grenadiere und leichte Infanteriekompanien trugen 'Flügel' auf den Schultern, manchmal mit gebüscheltel Kante; Offiziersflügel waren kunstvoll wattiert und mit Schnüren oder Ketten geschmückt.